COMPREHENSIVE RESEARCH
AND STUDY GUIDE

BLOOM'S
MAJOR
SHORT
STORY
WRITERS

Shirley

Jackson

EDITED AND WITH AN
INTRODUCTION BY HAROLD BLOOM

BLOOM'S MAJOR SHORT STORY WRITERS

Anton Chekhov

Joseph Conrad

Stephen Crane

William Faulkner

F. Scott Fitzgerald

Nathaniel Hawthorne

Ernest Hemingway

O. Henry

Shirley Jackson

Henry James

James Joyce

D. H. Lawrence

Jack London

Herman Melville

Flannery O'Connor

Edgar Allan Poe

Katherine Anne Porter

J. D. Salinger

John Steinbeck

Mark Twain

John Updike

Eudora Welty

BLOOM'S MAJOR WORLD POETS

Maya Angelou

Robert Browning

Geoffrey Chaucer

Samuel T. Coleridge

Dante

Emily Dickinson

John Donne

T. S. Eliot

Robert Frost

Homer

Langston Hughes

John Keats

John Milton

Sylvia Plath

Edgar Allan Poe

Poets of World War I

Shakespeare's Poems & Sonnets

Percy Shelley

Alfred, Lord Tennyson

Walt Whitman

William Wordsworth

William Butler Yeats

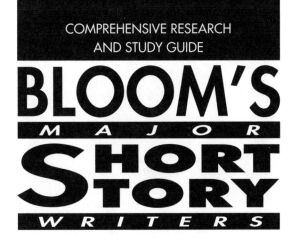

COMPREHENSIVE RESEARCH
AND STUDY GUIDE

BLOOM'S

MAJOR

SHORT
STORY

WRITERS

Shirley

Jackson

EDITED AND V   BLOOM

First Printing
1 3 5 7 9 8 6 4 2

Library of Congress Cataloging-in-Publication Data
applied for

ISBN 0-7910-5948-0

Chelsea House Publishers
1974 Sproul Road, Suite 400
Broomall, PA 19008-0914

The Chelsea House World Wide Web address is
http://www.chelseahouse.com

Contributing Editor: Aaron Tillman

Produced by: Robert Gerson Publisher's Services, Santa Barbara, CA

Contents

User's Guide

This volume is designed to present biographical, critical, and bibliographical information on the author's best-known or most important short stories. Following Harold Bloom's editor's note and introduction is a detailed biography of the author, discussing major life events and important literary accomplishments. A plot summary of each short story follows, tracing significant themes, patterns, and motifs in the work, and an annotated list of characters supplies brief information on the main characters in each story.

A selection of critical extracts, derived from previously published material from leading critics, analyzes aspects of each short story. The extracts consist of statements from the author, if available, early reviews of the work, and later evaluations up to the present. A bibliography of the author's writings (including a complete list of all books written, cowritten, edited, and translated), a list of additional books and articles on the author and the work, and an index of themes and ideas in the author's writings conclude the volume.

~

Harold Bloom is Sterling Professor of the Humanities at Yale University and Henry W. and Albert A. Berg Professor of English at the New York University Graduate School. He is the author of over 20 books, including *Shelley's Mythmaking* (1959), *The Visionary Company* (1961), *Blake's Apocalypse* (1963), *Yeats* (1970), *A Map of Misreading* (1975), *Kabbalah and Criticism* (1975), *Agon: Toward a Theory of Revisionism* (1982), *The American Religion* (1992), *The Western Canon* (1994), and *Omens of Millennium: The Gnosis of Angels, Dreams, and Resurrection* (1996). *The Anxiety of Influence* (1973) sets forth Professor Bloom's provocative theory of the literary relationships between the great writers and their predecessors. His most recent books include *Shakespeare: The Invention of the Human*, a 1998 National Book Award finalist, and *How to Read and Why*, which was published in 2000.

Professor Bloom earned his Ph.D. from Yale University in 1955 and has served on the Yale faculty since then. He is a 1985 MacArthur Foundation Award recipient, served as the Charles Eliot Norton Professor of Poetry at Harvard University in 1987–88, and has received honorary degrees from the universities of Rome and Bologna. In 1999, Professor Bloom received the prestigious American Academy of Arts and Letters Gold Medal for Criticism.

Currently, Harold Bloom is the editor of numerous Chelsea House volumes of literary criticism, including the series BLOOM'S NOTES, BLOOM'S MAJOR DRAMATISTS, BLOOM'S MAJOR NOVELISTS, MAJOR LITERARY CHARACTERS, MODERN CRITICAL VIEWS, MODERN CRITICAL INTERPRETATIONS, and WOMEN WRITERS OF ENGLISH AND THEIR WORKS.

Editor's Note

My Introduction discusses Shirley Jackson's best-known short story, "The Lottery," and questions whether the story, although commonly anthologized, will ultimately be regarded as canonical.

As there are some 23 Critical Views excerpted here, I will comment on a select few. Joan Wylie Hall considers "Charles" to be Jackson's funniest family drama.

Cleanth Brooks and Robert Penn Warren praise the author's construction of "The Lottery," and this section also includes the views of Shirley Jackson herself, and of her husband and editor, Stanley Edgar Hyman.

Judie Newman writes on the mother-daughter relationship in Jackson's short novel *The Haunting of Hill House*, after which Roberta Rubenstein explains how Eleanor Vance is willingly consumed by the evil force of Hill House. ❀

Introduction

HAROLD BLOOM

Only a few months before I wrote this Introduction, the Taliban in Kabul, Afghanistan, stoned to death a woman caught in adultery. As Islamic fundamentalists, the Taliban follow their interpretation of the Koran, itself based upon Jewish-Christian sources.

Shirley Jackson's famous story "The Lottery" is peculiarly horrifying because it is so artfully affectless. In what seems an upper New England setting, an annual ritual takes place. We are in a village so small that everyone appears to know everyone else, and the stoning to death of Mrs. Hutchinson has no relation to morality or to explicit religion. Perhaps that adds to the shock effect of "The Lottery," a story that depends upon tapping into a universal fear of arbitrary condemnation, and of sanctioned violence.

Like so many of Shirley Jackson's stories, "The Lottery" makes me brood upon the element of tendentiousness that renders her so problematic in aesthetic terms. Jackson always had too palpable a design upon her readers; her effects are as calculated as Poe's. Poe alas is inescapable: his nightmares were and are universal. This salvages him, despite the viciousness of his prose style, and absence of nuance in his work. Since he is greatly improved by translation (even into English), Poe has endured, and cannot be discarded, or even evaded.

"The Lottery," like most of Jackson's stories, is crisply written and cunningly plotted. But it scarcely bears rereading, which is (I think) the test for canonical literature. Jackson knows too well exactly what she is doing, and on rereading, so do we. You *can* learn certain rudiments of narration from "The Lottery," and yet the story's strict economy, which is its overt strength, is finally something of a stunt. It is as though we are at a magic show and we can see all the wires that ought to be invisible.

Literary judgment depends upon comparison, and so it is valid to contrast "The Lottery" to other stories that frighten us by relying upon archaic rituals. There is a long American tradition of Gothic narrative, whose masters include Hawthorne, Faulkner, and Flannery O'Connor. But these are masters and disturb us more profoundly than Jackson can, because they portray the complexities of character and personality without which we cannot permanently be moved. As fabulists, the masters of American Gothic carry us on a journey to the interior. Jackson certainly aspired to be more than an entertainer; her concern with sorceries, ancient and modern, was authentic and even pragmatic. But her art of narration stayed on the surface, and could not depict individual identities. Even "The Lottery" wounds you once, and once only. ❀

Biography of
Shirley Jackson

Shirley Hardie Jackson was born on December 14, 1919, in San Francisco, California. In 1923, her family moved to Burlingame, California, where Shirley attended public high school seven years later. It was during her high school years in California, 1930–1933, that Shirley began writing poetry and short fiction. In 1934, Shirley's family moved to Rochester, New York. Shirley finished her high school career at Brighton High in Rochester, where she was ranked in the top quarter of her class.

Jackson enrolled in a liberal arts program at the University of Rochester, where she remained until her withdrawal in 1936. She spent the next year at home, where she is believed to have written over a thousand words a day. In 1937, she entered Syracuse University. She originally planned to be a journalism major, but eventually changed to a dual major in English and Speech. Her first undergraduate story, "Janice," was published in the Syracuse University magazine. She was later appointed fiction editor of the campus humor periodical.

In 1939, Jackson won second prize in a university poetry contest. Soon after this, she met Stanley Edgar Hyman. She and Stanley went on to found and act as editors for a new literary magazine called *Spectre*. Shirley graduated from Syracuse in June 1940, and married Hyman immediately after graduation. Later that same year, the couple moved to New York City, where Stanley was appointed editorial assistant for *The New Republic*. Shirley Jackson's first national publication, "My Life With R. H. Macy," was published the following year in *The New Republic*.

In 1942, Shirley and Stanley's first child, Laurence, was born. The following year, she published the first of many stories in *The New Yorker*. Two years later, her story "Come Dance with Me in Ireland" was chosen for *Best American Short Stories, 1944*. In 1945, Shirley and Stanley moved to Bennington, Vermont, where Hyman began teaching at Bennington College. Shirley worked as a substitute teacher of the creative writing class until the birth of her second child, a daughter named Joanne.

In 1948, Jackson published her first novel, *The Road through the Wall*. That same year, seven of her short stories were published, including "Charles" and "The Lottery," and she gave birth to her third child, Sarah. Her second book, the collection of short stories *The Lottery, or The Adventures of James Harris*, was published in 1949. That same year, Stanley Hyman took a position with *The New Yorker* and they moved to Westport, Connecticut. Before the close of the year, the story "The Lottery" was included in *Prize Stories of 1949*.

In 1950, Jackson published six short stories in various magazines. The following year, *Hangsaman*, her second novel and third book, was published. Later that year, Shirley and Hyman moved back to Bennington, Vermont, where Barry, their fourth child, was born. It was also in 1951 that Jackson's story "The Summer People" was chosen for *Best American Short Stories, 1951*.

In 1952, "The Lottery" was adapted for television. In that same year, she published eleven stories, including "Night We All Had Grippe." *Life among the Savages*, a family chronicle, made it to print in 1953. It was in this year that "The Lottery" was first adapted for the stage. In 1954, her novel *The Bird's Nest* met critical acclaim. In 1956, *The Witchcraft of Salem Village* reached print, *The Bird's Nest* was adapted for film, and "One Ordinary Day With Peanuts" was selected for *Best American Short Stories, 1956*.

In 1957, *Raising Demons*, her second family chronicle, was published. The following year, *The Sundial* and the one-act play *The Bad Children* reached publication. *The Haunting of Hill House*, dedicated to Leonard Brown, came out in 1959. In 1961, her story "Louisa, Please" received the Edgar Allen Poe Award. In 1962, her novel *We Have Always Lived in the Castle* made it on the best-seller list, and was later named one of the year's "Ten Best Novels" by *Time* magazine.

In 1963, the successful film adaptation of *The Haunting* was released. That year, Jackson was hired to review children's books for *New York Herald Tribune*. In 1964, her story "Birthday Party" was selected for *Best American Short Stories, 1964*. That year, she was a member of the teaching staff at Breadloaf Writers' Conference.

In 1965, Syracuse University gave her the Arents Pioneer Medal for Outstanding Achievement. Illness prevented her from attending the ceremony. On August 8, 1965, Shirley Jackson died of heart failure.

The following year, *The Magic of Shirley Jackson*, a collection of her work edited by Stanley Edgar Hyman, was published. The play production of *We Have Always Lived in the Castle* opened on Broadway on October 20, 1966, and closed four days later. In 1968, *Come Along With Me*, a volume of work containing Jackson's unfinished novel, sixteen short stories, and three lectures—edited by Stanley Edgar Hyman—was published. ❀

Plot Summary of
"Charles"

"Charles," one of Shirley Jackson's highly acclaimed stories, opens as Laurie, the son of the woman who narrates the story, has just left for his first day in kindergarten. Laurie's mother tells how she watched him leave, knowing that an era of her life had ended. Laurie is depicted as an outspoken and confident boy. He enjoys telling stories about his experiences in school, particularly those involving a student named Charles, who has behavioral problems.

Each day, Laurie comes home from school and informs his parents about the misdeeds of Charles and the subsequent punishments this boy receives. Charles' actions have ranged from hitting the teacher to bouncing a see-saw onto a little girl's head, causing her to bleed. Laurie's parents grow increasingly interested in these stories. They begin to inquire about Charles regularly. After one particular incident, Laurie's parents ask what prompted Charles to act up, and Laurie responds with curious detail and nonchalance, saying that he "'wanted to color with green crayons so he hit the teacher and she spanked him and said nobody play with Charles but everybody did.'"

Following a week of increasingly horrific stories, Laurie's mother asks her husband if he thinks that kindergarten is too disturbing for their son. He responds that Laurie was bound to meet people like this eventually, so it might as well be now.

The ensuing Monday, Laurie comes home from school late, claiming that Charles was "'bad again.'" He says that Charles yelled in class and they made him stay after school, so all the other kids stayed with him. Laurie's mother asks her son to describe what Charles looks like. He says that Charles is bigger than him "'and he doesn't have any rubbers and he doesn't ever wear a jacket.'"

That Monday there is a parent-teacher meeting at the school. Though Laurie's mother had originally planned to go, she is forced to stay home with her sick baby. She deeply regrets that she won't get to meet Charles' mother. The next day, Laurie announces that someone came to visit their class. His mother and father instantly ask if the visitor was Charles' mother. Laurie tells them that it was a man who came to do exercises with them. He says that Charles didn't get to do exercises because he was fresh to the teacher's friend and that he kicked him. Laurie's father asks what they are going to do about this mischievous child. Laurie answers that they'll probably kick him out of school.

According to the narrative, the next few days are fairly ordinary: "Charles yelled during story hour and hit a boy in the stomach and made him cry." By the third week of kindergarten, Charles is "an institution" in Laurie's family. They start referring to ordinary hazards or mishaps as doing "a Charles." In the fourth and fifth week of school, the stories get increasingly less frequent; Charles has started to settle down. Laurie tells his parents that his teacher has even begun calling Charles her "little helper." Charles hands things out for her and helps her clean up. Laurie's parents are somewhat disappointed that there are fewer stories to hear at lunch, but they are confident that he will not be able to sustain this good behavior.

Laurie's mother announces that another PTA meeting is coming up, and this time she's going to find Charles' mother and see what happened to her child. That afternoon, Laurie comes home and reveals that Charles is at it again. He says that when he was handing out crayons—acting as the teacher's "little helper"—he told a girl to say a nasty word. When she repeated the word, the teacher washed her mouth out with soap. Laurie's father asks to hear the word, so Laurie whispers it in his father's ear. He is amazed that Charles got the girl to repeat it aloud.

The following Monday, Charles uttered the word himself, multiple times. As a result, the teacher washed his mouth out with soap. Charles also threw chalk. That night, Laurie's mother goes to the PTA meeting, eager to meet Charles' mother. During the meeting, she scrutinizes every parent in attendance, attempting to determine which is Charles' mother. Much to her dismay, no one looks haggard enough to be his parent, and no one mentions his name.

Following the meeting, Laurie's mother grabs some cake and tea and introduces herself to her son's kindergarten teacher. The teacher says that they're all interested in Laurie. The mother claims that her son really likes school and that he talks about it constantly. The teacher admits that Laurie had some trouble adjusting at first, but with the exception of a few lapses, he's been "a fine little helper."

Laurie's mother is surprised to hear the teacher say that her son has had trouble adjusting. She blames his difficulty on the influence of Charles, suggesting that she must have her hands full with him. The story ends with the teacher's bewildered reply: "'Charles?'" she questions. "'We don't have any Charles in the kindergarten.'" ❀

List of Characters in
"Charles"

Laurie has just started kindergarten when the story begins. Every day he returns at lunch and tells his parents about the misdeeds of a classmate named Charles. His parents become increasingly interested in these stories and eagerly await their son's return each day from school. When Laurie's mother goes to a PTA meeting and meets her son's teacher, she discovers that there is no such person as Charles and that the trouble-maker may, in fact, be Laurie.

Laurie's mother is the narrator of the story. She feels an era of her life coming to a close as her son, Laurie, heads off for his first day in kindergarten. She and her husband become increasingly involved in Laurie's stories about one of his troubled classmates, Charles. When she goes to a PTA meeting and meets her son's teacher, she discovers that Charles does not exist and that Laurie may be the troubled child.

Laurie's father relishes his son's stories about Charles. He insists that his wife find Charles' mother when she goes to the PTA meeting.

Laurie's kindergarten teacher meets Laurie's mother and tells her that her son has had some trouble adjusting. When Laurie's mother blames his adjustment problems on Charles, the teacher reveals that there is no Charles in her kindergarten class. ✿

Critical Views on
"Charles"

CHESTER E. EISINGER ON THE GOTHIC SPIRIT

[Chester E. Eisinger is the author of *Fiction of the Forties*. In this excerpt, Eisinger discusses how many of Jackson's characters, like Laurie in "Charles," possess a surprising capacity for horror.]

Many of the short stories in Shirley Jackson's *The Lottery, or The Adventures of James Harris* (1949) resemble closely the kind of new fiction written by Bowles, and by Capote too. Where Bowles is strident and melodramatic, she manages a low-keyed and quiet nihilism which is nonetheless almost as pervasive as his. Where both men force us to look into the uncovered face of evil, she quite matter of factly assumes its presence everywhere; indeed, her healthy-looking, apparently normal children reveal a particular appetite for contemplating violence and horror. Seemingly content to deal with ordinary experience in an ordinary way, she is always aware of the other side of consciousness, of the lurking figure, real or imagined, who leads her characters out into a strange nowhere. Her unpretentious and rather colorless prose is a suitable vehicle for the laconic expression of an equation of disintegration: as the culture seems to be going to pieces in some of these stories, so does the human personality. Her fiction is created out of this play on the incongruity between the ordinariness of her manner and the unreality of the reality that she perceives. Her dedication to a pessimistic view of experience is everywhere explicit, but occasionally it is obscured by the manipulation of her paradoxes.

—Chester E. Eisinger, *Fiction of the Forties* (Chicago: The University of Chicago Press, 1963): pp. 288–89.

LENEMAJA FRIEDMAN ON THE REAL CHARLES

[Lenemaja Friedman is a professor of English Literature at Columbus College. She has published short stories and reviewed several books for *Choice* magazine. In this excerpt, Friedman discusses the relationship between the real characters in Jackson's life and her fictional characters.]

The two Hyman children who move in with their parents are Laurie (Laurence) and Jannie (Joanne). Within the next six years, Sally (Sarah) is the next to appear; and last of all comes Barry. Because he is the oldest, Laurie is the central figure in most of the stories dealing with the children; and he is approximately nine years old when the book ends.

One of the first and the most famous of the anecdotes is the incident of "Charles." As Miss Jackson tells it, during Laurie's first few weeks in kindergarten, he came home every day to report the misdeeds of Charles, a little boy who caused little girls to say naughty words, who threw chalk, yelled in school, and not only kicked the gymnasium teacher, but also hit his own teacher. The family, duly impressed with the audaciousness of this Charles, was eager for Mrs. Hyman (Shirley Jackson) to meet his mother on Parent-Teachers' Association night. At the meeting, Mrs. Hyman searched the assembly for the suitably worn, frazzled-looking woman who would be the mother of such a boy. Having no success, she chatted instead with the teacher who mentioned that Laurie had had trouble adjusting to school, but now, with a few lapses, he has been doing well. In answer to Mrs. Hyman's question about Charles, the teacher looked puzzled. "Charles? . . . We don't have any Charles in the kindergarten."

The surprise ending with Laurie's being the culprit is more effective for reader interest than the actual situation; for there really was a cantankerous little boy named Charles who caused the teacher and the school authorities much grief and much hand wringing. This is the type of manipulation of fact that Miss Jackson uses; and, while it may deny a minor truth, it nevertheless makes a more entertaining story.

—Lenemaja Friedman, *Shirley Jackson* (Boston: Twayne Publishers, 1975): pp. 146–47.

[Judy Oppenheimer has been a reporter at *The Washington Post*, movie critic at the *Philadelphia Daily News*, and associate editor of the *Montgomery Sentinel*. Her writing has appeared in *Ms., The Village Voice*, and the *Manchester Guardian*. In this excerpt, Oppenheimer discusses the attention that many of Shirley Jackson's short stories received, including the "much anthologized" story "Charles."]

Her publishers, Farrar, Straus, ⟨. . .⟩ were frankly delighted ⟨with the success of "The Lottery"⟩ and moved quickly to capitalize on the sudden attention, making plans to issue a collection of Shirley's stories early in 1949. "The Lottery," of course, would double as title and featured presentation.

Shirley's productivity continued. Pregnancy, as usual, seemed to unleash even more energy. Barely a month after "The Lottery" appeared *Mademoiselle* published her wickedly funny family story, "Charles," about Laurie's experiences in kindergarten—a story which also used a shock ending, though of a very different sort, and which would eventually find its way into almost as many anthologies as "The Lottery."

In the story, Laurie—the fictional Laurie—takes to kindergarten right away, talking nonstop about the various terrible activities of a classmate, Charles, who kicks people, throws crayons, and gives vent to a number of off-color oaths. After a month, his mother, who has been worrying nervously about possible bad influences, finally meets the teacher. "You must have your hands full in that kindergarten, with Charles," she commiserates.

"Charles?" says the teacher. "We don't have any Charles in the kindergarten." (The tale, of course, was fiction, but according to many of Shirley's friends, not all that far from truth; Laurie could be an aggressive little boy. The odd thing was that Shirley *was* always worrying about bad influences on Laurie—while at the same time, as the story clearly shows, she knew her kid.)

Several other stories followed, appearing in various places. She also wrote "The Summer People," a tale of vacationers who come up against the brutal justice of a small New England town, which impressed Stanley—"not only seems scarier than lottery but is probably better," he wrote Williams, in August—but no one else, at least then: it was rejected by several magazines. (Stanley, as usual, had the better eye—three years later June Mirken, who was then fiction editor of *Charm* magazine, spotted it on a visit and grabbed it fast. It made *The Best American Short Stories, 1951*.)

—Judy Oppenheimer, *Private Demons: The Life of Shirley Jackson* (New York: Fawcett Columbine, 1988): p. 132.

JOAN WYLIE HALL ON REBELLIOUS SONS AND DAUGHTERS

[Joan Wylie Hall has been an instructor of English at the University of Notre Dame and the University of Mississippi. She has written scholarly works on Ruth McEnery Stuart, Willa Cather, Marilyn French, and Shirley Jackson. In this excerpt, Hall speaks on the story "Charles" as perhaps the funniest account of motherhood in the collection.]

The centerpiece in the largest group of stories, "Charles" presents the book's most humorous treatment of the beleaguered mother. First published as fiction in *Mademoiselle*, the semi-autobiographical story was later incorporated into Jackson's family chronicle, *Life Among the Savages*. Next to "The Lottery" "Charles" is the most frequently anthologized piece from Jackson's collection, and probably for a similar reason: both end with an unforgettable scene that suddenly forces the reader to reconsider the whole preceding sequence of events. The mild tension of the opening, as the narrator's son Laurie sets off for kindergarten, ending "an era of my life," hardly prepares us for the startling denouement. But, as frequently happens in Jackson's stories, the tension so steadily increases that the central character, Laurie's mother, is finally forced to take action.

"Charles" is the third story in a row to stage the family drama around the kitchen table. This is the center to which the newly independent Laurie returns each noon to report on the latest exploits of his classmate, the Charles of Jackson's title. Like the children in "The Witch" and "The Renegade," Laurie relishes reporting acts of violence and cruelty. He is entertained rather than upset when Charles hits the teacher, kicks the teacher's friend, or punches a boy in the stomach. Laurie grins "enormously," jokes with his father, and laughs "insanely" between accounts of the morning's events. Unusual for a father in *The Lottery*, Laurie's is not only present, but also supportive of his wife, whose questions and reactions are typically more urgent than his own. When she asks her husband whether kindergarten might be too "unsettling" for Laurie, he assures her everything will be all right.

Like most of Jackson's women, the unnamed mother tries to contain her fears. She responds "heartily," for example, when Laurie describes Charles's refusal to do exercises. But she also becomes "passionately" intent on meeting Charles's mother, and she goes to the neutral ground of a PTA assembly alone, no husband by her side. Once there, she is restless, "scanning each comfortable matronly face, trying to determine which one hid the secret of Charles. None of them looked to me haggard enough." She resembles the questing women in "The Daemon Lover" and "The Renegade" as she cautiously approaches Laurie's teacher for help, and her quest too ends in humiliation. Unexpectedly learning that Laurie has had some adjustment problems, the surprised narrator quickly assigns the blame to Charles. The first protagonist in *The Lottery* to laugh, she sympathizes with the teacher for having her hands full with Charles in her class, but she laughs alone. With the teacher's closing words, another of Jackson's women is abruptly enlightened, and speechless as a result: "'Charles?' she said. 'We don't have any Charles in the kindergarten.'" The narrator had studied every face but her own for signs of the worry she bears as the anxious mother who unknowingly harbors "the secret of Charles."

In the last three stories in the second group, Jackson broadens her focus on families to include a third generation. Grandmothers are powerful forces in each case, and the challenges issued them by their children or grandchildren form a central conflict in all three. In several ways resembling "Charles," "Afternoon in Linen" portrays Harriet, a 10-year-old who deceives her grandmother, embarrassing the woman in front of others. The opening sentence depicts a peaceful scene, a cool room with a view of flowering bushes, that in no way prepares for the final moment of humiliation. An allusion later in the paragraph, however, anticipates the reversal. The two women and two children who gather in the formal room all wear linen, a coincidence that quickly leads the precocious Harriet to identify with an episode from *Through the Looking-Glass*, a fantasy based on reversals. Her grandmother, dressed in white, reminds her of Lewis Carroll's gentleman in white paper, and "I'm a gentleman all dressed in pink paper, she thought."

—Joan Wylie Hall, *Shirley Jackson: A Study of the Short Fiction* (New York: Twayne Publishers, 1993): pp. 27–28.

Plot Summary of
"The Lottery"

"The Lottery," Shirley Jackson's most controversial and acclaimed story, opens on a clear, sunny summer morning at the end of June, as the people of a village begin gathering in the public square, preparing for the town's annual lottery. In true Shirley Jackson fashion, suspense is built around the unknown nature of this particular lottery. The narrative informs the reader that in some towns, the lottery takes two days, but there are only three hundred people in this particular village, so the entire event takes under two hours.

The narrative first introduces three boys from the village, Bobby Martin, Harry Jones, and Dickie Dellacroix, as they fill their pockets with stones and make a great pile in the corner of the square. While this is taking place, the men from the village gather toward the front. Keeping the particulars of the lottery ambiguous, Jackson fills the narrative with somber overtones, describing how the men stand quietly together, "away from the pile of stones," smiling but never laughing. "The women, wearing faded house dresses and sweaters," come shortly after the men.

The lottery is an annual event and is hosted by Mr. Summers, a man who earns pity from the townsfolk because his wife is mean and they have no children. Mr. Summers arrives at the square carrying a black box. For countless years, this exact box has been used to hold the slips of paper from which the names are drawn. Though the original ornaments used for the lottery were lost long ago, "the black box now resting on the stool had been put into use even before Old Man Warner, the oldest man in town, was born."

Mr. Martin and his elder son Baxter take the responsibility of holding the box while Mr. Summers stirs the papers with his hand. The slips of paper had been made up the evening before by Mr. Summers and Mr. Graves, and then locked in a safe at Mr. Summers' coal company.

The narrative describes the process that Mr. Summers goes through while preparing for the lottery. He has to make up lists of every member of every family, noting the head of each household.

Then there is the "proper swearing-in of Mr. Summers by the postmaster, as the official of the lottery." The narrative consistently relates back to the way events had been run, referring to the forgotten rituals of years past.

As the preliminary events are just about finished, Mrs. Hutchinson hurries into the town square and slides into the crowd, claiming to have forgotten that today is the day for the lottery. She makes her way through the crowd until she is up in the front, standing next to her husband and family. Once Mrs. Hutchinson takes her place, Mr. Summers tells the crowd that he'd like to start the proceedings and asks if anyone is missing. Someone from the crowd informs him that Clyde Dunbar broke his leg and that his wife will be drawing for him.

Mr. Summers clears his throat and picks up his list. A "sudden hush" falls on the crowd. He instructs the heads of each family to come up as they are called and take a slip out of the black box. He reminds them that they are to wait with the folded slip until everyone has drawn. Though Mr. Summers is careful to explain all the details, the crowd, having gone through the ritual many times before, scarcely listens to the directions. They stand nervously, "wetting their lips, not looking around." The heads of each household are called forward alphabetically to receive their slips of paper. As they approach Mr. Summers, they grin "humorlessly and nervously." While their names are being called, the narrative chronicles a conversation between Mrs. Graves and Mrs. Delacroix, both of whom feel as though the last lottery had just taken place. The narrative shifts to a conversation between Mr. Adams and Old Man Warner. Mr. Adams says that in the North village there has been talk of abandoning the lottery. "'Pack of crazy fools,'" Old Man Warner replies, claiming that nothing is good enough for the younger generations.

Once everyone has a slip of paper, including Old Man Warner, who proudly states that this is his seventy-seventh year in the lottery, the men open their slips. Another great hush falls over the crowd, before the women start asking aloud "'Who is it? Who's got it?'" It is revealed that Bill Hutchinson has the pertinent slip of paper. The crowd looks awkwardly at the Hutchinson family. Bill looks solemnly down at the paper. His wife, Tessie, starts to yell at Mr. Summers, claiming that the proceedings weren't conducted fairly.

The women around Mrs. Hutchinson try to calm her down, saying that they all took the same chance. Then Bill Hutchinson turns to his wife and tells her to shut up.

Once the shock has settled, Mr. Summers instructs Bill Hutchinson to draw for his family, asking if there are any other households living with them. Mrs. Hutchinson yells out that Don and Eva should be forced to draw, but Mr. Summers reminds her that daughters always draw with their husbands' families. After formally determining that Bill is the head of the household, Mr. Summers asks him to list his children and family members. He recites aloud that in addition to himself, there are his children Bill Jr., Nancy, and Dave, and his wife Tessie.

Mr. Summers instructs Harry Graves to place a slip of paper for each member of the Hutchinson family in the black box. One slip is marked—the same slip that Bill Hutchinson had drawn from the box originally. Mrs. Hutchinson says again, in a defeated voice, that she thinks they should start over, that the proceedings weren't fair. Mr. Summers tells each member of the Hutchinson family to take a slip of paper and keep it folded by their side until everyone has drawn. Mr. Graves helps little Davy to take out his paper. Then Nancy, who is twelve, takes a slip and hears the tense sighs from the girls in her class. Bill Jr., Tessie, and Bill Sr. each grab a slip of folded paper. The children open their papers first, each revealing a blank slip. Bill opens his paper to reveal yet another blank slip. Mr. Summers makes the inevitable declaration "'It's Tessie.'"

Bill Hutchinson has to force the slip of paper out of his wife's clenched hands. It has a black spot on it, "the black spot Mr. Summers had made the night before with the heavy pencil in the coal-company office." Bill holds it up. There is a stir in the crowd.

The focus shifts to the pile of stones that the boys had made earlier. The townsfolk have begun to pick from the pile, each member holding a rock of a different shape and size. Tessie is led to the center of a cleared space. She holds out her hands, gesturing desperately to the villagers. "'It isn't fair,'" she says, before a stone hits her in the side of the head. Old Man Warner rallies the town folks to attack. "'It isn't fair, it isn't right,'" Tessie screams one last time before everyone is "upon her." ✾

List of Characters in
"The Lottery"

Bill Hutchinson is the head of the Hutchinson family. He draws the initial dreaded slip of paper from the black box. He tells his wife to be quiet when she protests the outcome, and allows the ritual of the lottery to go on without protest.

Tessie Hutchinson is Bill Hutchinson's wife. She comes late to the lottery, claiming to have forgotten that it was the day for this strange event. She protests the proceedings after her husband picks the dreaded ticket. She is stoned to death at the end of the story.

Mr. Summers has been the host of the lottery for many years.

Old Man Warner is the oldest man in town. He has been involved in the lottery for seventy-seven years. He gets upset when Mr. Adams suggests that other towns are thinking of giving up the lottery. He believes that things should stay the way they are.

Mr. Adams has a conversation with Old Man Warner during the drawing and tells him that other towns have considered giving up the lottery.

Mr. Martin and *Baxter Martin* hold down the black box which contains the slips of paper for the lottery drawing.

Harry Graves is the postmaster who swears in Mr. Summers as the official host. He helps little Davy Hutchinson with his ticket.

Mrs. Graves has a conversation with Mrs. Delacroix about how last year's lottery seemed to have just taken place.

Mrs. Delacroix has a conversation with Mrs. Graves about how last year's lottery seemed to have just taken place. She tells Tessie Hutchinson to be a sport when she starts complaining about the proceedings.

Nancy Hutchinson is the twelve-year-old daughter of Bill and Tessie. Her classmates gasp when she draws a slip from the black box.

Bill Hutchinson Jr. is the son of Bill and Tessie Hutchinson.

Dave Hutchinson is the youngest child of Bill and Tessie Hutchinson.

Bobby Martin, Harry Jones, and *Dickie Delacroix* are the first characters introduced. They are gathering stones when the story opens. ❀

Critical Views on
"The Lottery"

CLEANTH BROOKS AND ROBERT PENN WARREN ON THE STORY AS SOCIAL COMMENTARY

[Cleanth Brooks (1906–1994) was the Gray Professor Emeritus of Rhetoric at Yale University. He wrote more than twenty books, including *Literary Criticism: A Short History* (1957). Robert Penn Warren (1905–1989) was an American poet and novelist who received the Pulitzer Prize twice for poetry (*Promises,* 1957; *Now and Then: Poems,* 1978) and once for fiction (*All the King's Men,* 1946). Brooks and Warren collaborated on such influential books as *Understanding Fiction* (1943) and co-founded the *Southern Review.* In this excerpt, they discuss how "The Lottery" deals with issues relevant to the time.]

"The Lottery," then, deals indeed with live issues and issues relevant to our time. If we hesitate to specify a particular "point" that the story makes, it is not because the story is vague and fuzzy, but rather because its web of observations about human nature is too subtle and too complex to be stated in one or two brief maxims.

What requires a little further attention is a problem of a quite different sort: how does this story differ from a tract or a treatise on human nature? Are we actually justified in calling it a piece of fiction?

An answer to these questions might run like this: This is obviously not a tract or merely an essay. The village is made to exist for us; the characters of Old Man Warner and Mr. Summers and Mrs. Hutchinson do come alive. They are not fully developed, to be sure, and there is a sense in which even the personality of the victim is finally subservient to the "point" to be made and is not developed in its own right and for its own sake. But, as we have said, this is not a "naked parable"—and the fact that we get an impression of a real village and real people gives the sense of grim terror.

The fictional form thus justifies itself by making vivid and forceful what would otherwise have to be given prosaically and undramatically. But it does something else that is very important: it provides a special shaping of the reader's attitude toward the climactic event and toward that from which the climactic event stems. The reader's attitude has been moulded very carefully from the very beginning. Everything in the story has been devised to let us know how we are to "take" the final events in the story.

The very fact that an innocent woman is going to be stoned to death by her friends and neighbors and that this is to happen in an American small town during our own present day of enlightenment requires a special preparation. The apparently fantastic nature of the happening means that everything else in the story must be made plausible, down-to-earth, sensible, commonplace, everyday. We must be made to feel that what is happening on this June morning is perfectly credible. Making it seem credible will do two things: it will increase the sense of shock when we suddenly discover what is really going on, but it will ultimately help us to believe that what the story asserts does come to pass. In general, then, the horror of the ending is counter-balanced by the dry, even cheery, atmosphere of the scene. This contrast between the matter-of-factness and the cheery atmosphere, on one side, and the grim terror, on the other, gives us a dramatic shock. But it also indicates that the author's point in general has to do with the awful doubleness of the human spirit—a doubleness that expresses itself in the blended good neighborliness and cruelty of the community's action. The fictional form, therefore, does not simply "dress up" a specific comment on human nature. The fictional form actually gives point and definition to the social commentary.

—Cleanth Brooks and Robert Penn Warren, *Understanding Fiction* (New York: Appleton-Century-Crofts, 1959): pp. 75–76.

⊗

STANLEY EDGAR HYMAN ON SHIRLEY JACKSON

[Stanley Edgar Hyman was Shirley Jackson's husband. He and his wife founded the literary magazine *Spectre,* and he later worked as an editor for *The New Republic* and *The New*

People often expressed surprise at the difference between Shirley Jackson's appearance and manner, and the violent and terrifying nature of her fiction. Thus many of the obituaries played up the contrast between a "motherly-looking" woman, gentle and humorous, and that "chillingly horrifying short story 'The Lottery'" and similar works. When Shirley Jackson, who was my wife, published two light-hearted volumes about the spirited doings of our children, *Life Among the Savages* and *Raising Demons*, it seemed to surprise people that the author of her grim and disturbing fiction should be a wife and mother at all, let alone a gay and apparently happy one.

This seems to me to be the most elementary misunderstanding of what a writer is and how a writer works, on the order of expecting Herman Melville to be a big white whale. Shirley Jackson, like many writers, worked in a number of forms and styles, and she exploited each of them as fully as she could. When she wrote a novel about the disintegration of a personality, *The Bird's Nest*, it was fittingly macabre and chilling; when she wrote a funny account of "My Life with R. H. Macy," it was fittingly uproarious. Everything she wrote was written with absolute seriousness and integrity, with all the craft she could muster; nothing was ever careless or dashed off; but she did not believe that a serious purpose necessarily required a serious tone.

Shirley Jackson wrote in a variety of forms and styles because she was, like everyone else, a complex human being, confronting the world in many different roles and moods. She tried to express as much of herself as possible in her work, and to express each aspect as fully and purely as possible. While she wanted the fullest self-expression consistent with the limits of literary form, at the same time she wanted the widest possible audience for that self-expression; she wanted, in short, a public, sales, "success." For her entire adult life she regarded herself as a professional writer, one who made a living by the craft of writing, and as she did not see that vocation as incompatible with being a wife and mother, so she did not see her dedication to art as incompatible with producing art in salable forms. In this, as in other respects, she was curiously old-fashioned.

Despite a fair degree of popularity—reviews of her books were generally enthusiastic, reprints and foreign publications were numerous, and her last two novels, *The Haunting of Hill House* and *We Have Always Lived in the Castle*, became modest best-sellers—Shirley Jackson's work and its nature and purpose have been very little understood. Her fierce visions of dissociation and madness, of alienation and withdrawal, of cruelty and terror, have been taken to be personal, even neurotic, fantasies. Quite the reverse: they are a sensitive and faithful anatomy of our times, fitting symbols for our distressing world of the concentration camp and the Bomb. She was always proud that the Union of South Africa banned "The Lottery," and she felt that *they* at least understood the story.

—Stanley Edgar Hyman, *The Magic of Shirley Jackson*, ed. Stanley Edgar Hyman (New York: Farrar, Straus and Giroux, 1965): pp. vii–viii.

LENEMAJA FRIEDMAN ON RESPONSE TO THE STORY

[Lenemaja Friedman is a professor of English Literature at Columbus College. She has published short stories and reviewed several books for *Choice* magazine. In this excerpt, Friedman speaks on the flood of letters that followed the original publication of the story.]

One of the ancient practices that modern man deplores as inhumanly evil is the annual sacrifice of a scapegoat or a god-figure for the benefit of the community. Throughout the ages, from ancient Rome and Greece to the more recent occurrences in African countries, sacrifices in the name of a god of vegetation were usual and necessary, the natives felt, for a fertile crop. Somewhere along the way, the sacrifice of a human for the sins of the people—to drive evil from themselves—became linked with the ritual of the vegetation god. In Mexico, among the Aztecs, the victims impersonated the particular gods for a one-year period before being put to death; death came then by the thrust of a knife into the breast and the immediate extraction of the heart. In Athens, each year in May, at the festival of the Thargelia, two victims, a man and a woman, were led out of the city and stoned to death. Death by stoning was one of the accepted and more popular methods of dispatching ceremonial victims.

But modern man considers such practices barbaric and, therefore, alien to his civilized behavior. For this reason, many persons were puzzled and shocked by "The Lottery." After its appearance in the June 28, 1948, issue of *The New Yorker*, a flood of mail—hundreds of letters—deluged both the editorial offices in New York and the post office in Bennington. No *New Yorker* story had ever received such a response. Of the many letters received, as Miss Jackson recalled, only thirteen spoke kindly to her; and those were from friends. Three main characteristics dominated the letters: bewilderment, speculation, and old-fashioned abuse. "The general tone of the early letters was a kind of wide-eyed shocked innocence. People at first were not so much concerned with what the story meant: what they wanted to know was where these lotteries were held, and whether they could go there and watch." Later, after the story had been anthologized, televised, and dramatized, the tone of the letters became more polite, but people still wondered what the story meant.

She had conceived the story idea, she said, on a fine June morning as she was returning from a trip to the grocery store and was pushing uphill the stroller containing her daughter and the day's groceries. Having the idea well in mind, she wrote the story so easily that the finished copy was almost the same word for word as the rough draft. Her agent, she recalls, did not care for the story; nor was the fiction editor of *The New Yorker* particularly impressed; however, the magazine was going to buy it. When Mr. Harold Ross, then editor of the magazine, indicated that the story might be puzzling to some people and asked if she would care to enlarge upon its meaning, she refused. But later, in response to numerous requests, she made the following statement, which appeared in the July 22 issue of the *San Francisco Chronicle*: "Explaining just what I had hoped the story to say is very difficult. I suppose, I hoped, by setting a particularly brutal ancient rite in the present and in my own village to shock the story's readers with a graphic dramatization of the pointless violence and general inhumanity in their own lives."

Several of Miss Jackson's friends had intimated that the village characters were modeled after actual persons in Bennington; but, if so, she took pains to disguise the fact. The names are plain, solid-sounding: Adams, Warner, Dunbar, Martin, Hutchinson, etc. The name Mr. Summers is particularly suitable for sunny, jovial Joe Summers; it emphasizes the surface tone of the piece and underscores the ultimate irony. Mr. Graves—the postmaster and the assistant to Mr. Summers in the administration of the lottery—has a name that might well signify the tragic undercurrent, which does not become meaningful until the end of the story. As in the other stories designating the presence of evil even in the least likely persons, such as in sweet old ladies, the reader discovers the blight in this deceptively pleasant community. In fact, much of the horror stems from the discrepancy between the normal outward appearance of the village life and its people and the heinous act these people commit in the guise of tradition.

—Lenemaja Friedman, *Shirley Jackson* (Boston: Twayne Publishers, 1975): pp. 63–64.

※

A. R. COULTHARD ON THE GRIM VIEW OF HUMAN NATURE

[A. R. Coulthard was a literary scholar at Appalachian State University. Coulthard's work has appeared in various literary journals, including *The Explicator*. In this excerpt, Coulthard discusses why so little has been written on the story, despite its wide circulation.]

Little has been written about "The Lottery," possibly the most widely known American short story. Perhaps that is because the story seems such a transparent attack on blind obedience to tradition that little or no exegesis is necessary, a reading usually encouraged by discussion questions accompanying this much-anthologized story. But "The Lottery" is not an assault on mindless, cultural conformity. It is a grim, even nihilistic, parable of the evil inherent in human nature.

It is not that the ancient custom of human sacrifice makes the villagers behave cruelly, but that their thinly veiled cruelty keeps the custom alive. Savagery fuels evil tradition, not vice versa. This is no chicken-egg question, but a fact evident from the text. From the beginning, the people display no genuine human community, no real bond of love. Considering that one of them could die within the hour, a possibility made more likely by the small number of potential victims, Tessie Hutchinson's tapping her friend Mrs. Delacroix "on the arm as a farewell" hardly seems a sign of sisterly concern. A short time later, it is Mrs. Delacroix who "selected a stone so large she had to pick it up with both hands" when her "friend" Tessie has become the scapegoat. In spite of such communal gestures as the crowd's separating "good-humoredly" to let Mrs. Hutchinson through, the villagers are looking forward to the slaughter, overtly so in the case of the children: "Bobby Martin had already stuffed his pockets full of stones, and the other boys soon followed his example, selecting the smoothest and roundest stones," the ones best for accurate throwing.

Old Man Warner is usually taken to be the most allegorically evil devotee of custom, but he is merely the most honest. He is also the only villager who seems to believe in the supposed original purpose of the sacrifice: "Lottery in June, corn be heavy soon," he intones. The others are willing to risk their own lives for the sheer pleasure of an unpunished annual killing. Mr. Adams and his wife mildly oppose the lottery by telling Old Man Warner that some villages are giving it up, but when it comes time for the stoning, "Steve Adams was in the front of the crowd." Such heavy-handed ironic twists imply that there is no such thing as communal love, or even sympathy, in the human heart.

The soullessness of Tessie Hutchinson even denies the myth of family love. When her family is chosen to supply the victim, Jackson pushes Tessie's survival instinct to the most shameful level by having her turn on her own flesh and blood. Tessie desperately tries to improve her odds for survival by defying tradition and adding her married daughter to the killing pool: "'There's Don and Eva,' Mrs. Hutchinson yelled. 'Make *them* take their chance.'" Tessie thinks, "It wasn't *fair*," only because another family was not selected, and her husband "regretfully" agrees, for he too could be the final choice. Even the children of Tessie's household share this unconcern for the other family members. When they draw their slips, "Nancy and Bill, Jr., opened theirs at the same time, and both beamed and laughed" because neither is chosen to die.

—A. R. Coulthard, "Jackson's 'The Lottery,'" *The Explicator* 48, no. 3 (Spring 1990): pp. 226–27.

※

SHIRLEY JACKSON ON THE CONTROVERSY SURROUNDING THE STORY

[In this essay, Shirley Jackson describes the anxiety that followed the publication of the story.]

On the morning of June 28, 1948, I walked down to the post office in our little Vermont town to pick up the mail. I was quite casual about it, as I recall—I opened the box, took out a couple of bills and a letter or two, talked to the postmaster for a few minutes, and left, never supposing that it was the last time for months that I was to pick up the mail without an active feeling of panic. By the next week I had had to change my mailbox to the largest one in the post office, and casual conversation with the postmaster was out of the question, because he wasn't speaking to me. June 28, 1948, was the day *The New Yorker* came out with a story of mine in it. It was not my first published story, nor my last, but I have been assured over and over that if it had been the only story I ever wrote or published, there would be people who would not forget my name.

I had written the story three weeks before, on a bright June morning when summer seemed to have come at last, with blue skies and warm sun and no heavenly signs to warn me that my morning's work was anything but just another story. The idea had come to me while I was pushing my daughter up the hill in her stroller—it was, as I say, a warm morning, and the hill was steep, and beside my daughter the stroller held the day's groceries—and perhaps the effort of that last fifty yards up the hill put an edge to the story; at any rate, I had the idea fairly clearly in my mind when I put my daughter in her playpen and the frozen vegetables in the refrigerator, and, writing the story, I found that it went quickly and easily, moving from beginning to end without pause. As a matter of fact, when I read it over later I decided that except for one or two minor corrections, it needed no changes, and the story I finally typed up and sent off to my agent the next day was almost word for word the original draft. This, as any writer of stories can tell you, is not a usual thing. All I know is that when I came to read the story over I felt strongly that I didn't want to fuss with it. I didn't think it was perfect, but I didn't want to fuss with it. It was, I thought, a serious, straightforward story, and I was pleased and a little surprised at the ease with which it had been written; I was reasonably proud of it, and hoped that my agent would sell it to some magazine and I would have the gratification of seeing it in print.

My agent did not care for the story, but—as she said in her note at the time—her job was to sell it, not to like it. She sent it at once to *The New Yorker*, and about a week after the story had been written I received a telephone call from the fiction editor of *The New Yorker*; it was quite clear that he did not really care for the story, either, but *The New Yorker* was going to buy it. He asked for one change—that the date mentioned in the story be changed to coincide with the date of the issue of the magazine in which the story would appear, and I said of course. He then asked, hesitantly, if I had any particular interpretation of my own for the story; Mr. Harold Ross, then the editor of *The New Yorker*, was not altogether sure that he understood the story, and wondered if I cared to enlarge upon its meaning. I said no. Mr. Ross, he said, thought that the story might be puzzling to some people, and in case anyone telephoned the magazine, as sometimes happened, or wrote in asking about the story, was there anything in particular I wanted them to say? No, I said, nothing in particular; it was just a story I wrote.

—Shirley Jackson, "The Morning of June 28, 1948, and 'The Lottery,'" in *The Story and its Writer: An Introduction to Short Fiction*, ed. Ann Charters (New York: Bedford Books, 1991): pp. 1458–59.

GAYLE WHITTIER ON MALE AND FEMALE ROLES IN THE STORY

[Gayle Whittier is a professor at SUNY Binghamton, where she teaches both literature and creative writing. She has published fiction in several magazines including *Ploughshares, TriQuarterly*, and *The Massachusetts Review*. In this excerpt, Whittier discusses the existence of male dominance throughout the story.]

Throughout the lottery process, male dominance—patriarchy's choice, however "blind"—is interpreted in a traditional way, as a burden rather than as a privilege. There is an air of duty and "good form" about the men as a group, and when Summers and Graves ask for help with the black box, a reluctance dignifies their sacrificial purpose. "... when Mr. Summers said, 'Some of you fellows want to give me a hand?' there was a hesitation before two men, Mr. Martin and his oldest son, Baxter, came forward to hold the box steady...." Such restraint continues to the end of the account. It is a man, Mr. Summers, who urges, "All right, folks ... Let's finish quickly," and *no* man is seen holding stones or actually stoning Tessie, though two women are presented as armed. A narrative whitewash covers patriarchal order.

But if the ordering of the lottery is patriarchal, its ancient purpose of human sacrifice in the name of crop fertility remains associated with the matriarchal worship of earth goddesses in an archaic time. Significantly, the men, seemingly reluctant yet duty-bound to perform the ceremony, relish its actual bloodshedding less than either women or uninitiated boys.

> Bobby Martin had already stuffed his pockets full of stones, and the other boys soon followed his example, selecting the smoothest and roundest stones; Bobby and Harry Jones and Dickie Dellacroix—the villagers pronounced this name "Dellacroy"—eventually made a great pile of stones in one corner of the square and guarded it aginst the raids of other boys. The girls stood aside, talking....

Here we see how the gender roles already marked in childhood, the boys' territorial protectiveness and the girls' exclusion, begin. But the boys' eager and childish cruelty will turn into the sober reluctance of their fathers, whereas the childish apartness of the girls will become the grown women's blood lust. For if the daughters stand apart, the mothers do not. It is Mrs. Delacroix who is first seen, stone in hand, about to cast it, and Mrs. Dunbar who, despite infirmity, tries to keep up with her.

> Mrs. Delacroix selected a stone so large she had to pick it up with both hands, and turned to Mrs. Dunbar. "Come on," she said, "Hurry up." Mrs. Dunbar had small stones in both hands, and she said, gasping for breath, "I can't run at all. You'll have to go ahead and I'll catch up with you."

To put it simply, women "grow up" to become like boys, immature men. It follows patriarchally that men not only can, but *must* control women if the appearance of "due process" and ritual form is to veneer the savagery of the stoning.

At first male control over women is silent and patient, as when Bill Hutchinson seems to ignore his wife's first protests. When she persists, he takes charge verbally, saying, "Shut up, Tessie." His *commandment* alone, however, fails to control her, so that, as she disturbs the ritual by refusing to show her black-marked slip of paper, he forces it out of her hand. Male force, then, is presented as "justified" by female dissent, even as male order both accommodates and keeps in check the ritual of goddess worship now obsolete, but, tragically, still followed.

—Gayle Whittier, "'The Lottery' as Misogynist Parable," in *Women's Studies* 18, no. 4 (1991): pp. 356–57.

⊗

NATHAN CERVO ON TESSIE AS SCAPEGOAT

[Nathan Cervo was a literary scholar at Franklin Pierce College. His work has appeared in various literary journals, including *The Explicator*. In this excerpt, Cervo offers a Christian interpretation of the story.]

The idea of the scapegoat is a commonplace of the criticism expended on "The Lottery." It is fitted within the sociological context of the archetypal fall guy or else raises questions concerning Original Sin and mankind's need to expiate sin either through personal suffering or vicariously. Clearly, the premises of "The Lottery" put Rousseau's benign sentimentality to rout; they are closely allied, in effect, with those of Curzio Malaparte's *La Pelle* (*The Skin*) because, when the chips are down, everybody wants just one thing—to save his own skin.

Those are the anti-Romantic premises of the story; but there is another premise, that evinced by the "Delacroix"/ "Dellacroy" dialectic. This premise builds upon and refers to the Day of Atonement lottery, most particularly as practiced in the days of Jesus. That lottery involved two goats; namely, the scapegoat (the goat that was not sacrificed) and the goat to be sacrificed to Jehovah as a sin offering. This latter goat was customarily hurled down a rocky precipice (hence, the twin motifs of stoning and the implicit idea, in Jackson's story, of Jehovah *qua* mountain baal—in keeping with Freud's view of Jehovah as expressed in *Moses and Monotheism*). The sacrificed goat "went rolling and falling down, he did not reach halfway down the mountain, before he became separated limb from limb." Meagher goes on to observe: "Bloody, torn, mangled, smashed on the rocks far below, lay the sinless victim with the sins of Israel on him, a striking image of the bloody body of the dead Christ with the sins of all mankind on Him."

But what is more central to this explication is the following paragraph from Meagher, who cites *Yomah*:

> "Now the high priest comes to the front of the altar, and a priest holds out to him the gold box, wherein are the "lots," on one is written: "For Jehovah," on the other "For Azazael." The Segan is on his right, the head of the family of priests serving that week on his left. If that of Jehovah was taken out by his right hand, the Segan says to him: "My Lord the high priest, raise thy right hand." If that of Jehovah was taken out by his left hand, the head of the family says: "My Lord the high priest, raise thy left hand." He placed the lots on the two goats saying: "To Jehovah, a sin offering." "For Azazael the scapegoat." The whole assembly responded with a mighty voice: "Blessed be the name of His Kingdom's glory forever."

In this historical and anthropological light, it is clear that Mrs. Hutchinson, whose "lot" it is to be stoned to death, is not a scapegoat figure. She is a parodic Christ-figure, slain to appease a demonic entity that is the personification of involuted (perhaps even self-consciously elaborated) ignorance masquerading as primitivistic piety. As metonymic extrapolation of her society, she is to be more properly thought of as a scapegrace.

—Nathan Cervo, "Jackson's 'The Lottery,'" *The Explicator* 50, no. 3 (Spring 1992): pp. 183–84.

JAY A. YARMOVE ON SYMBOLISM IN THE STORY

[Jay A. Yarmove has been a literary scholar and educator at the University of Cincinnati. His work has appeared in various literary journals, including *The Explicator*. In this excerpt, Yarmove discusses the significance of the names in the story.]

Not only do time and place bear important clues as to the allegorical meaning of "The Lottery," but the very names of the characters are laden with significance. The prominent names—Summers, Adams, Graves, Warner, Delacroix, and (most obviously) Tessie Hutchinson—have much to tell us. For the season of the lottery is summer, and the larger scope of this work encompasses mankind in general (for instance, "Adam" means "man" in Hebrew). "Graves" sounds a somber, forewarning note of what will happen to Tessie, and the oldest man in town, Old Man Warner (the others have either died or been killed off) warns us about the primordial function of the lottery, which is to ensure fertility: "Used to be a saying about 'Lottery in June, corn be heavy soon.'" Mrs. Delacroix's name alludes to the pseudo-crucifixion of Tessie.

It is the irony that lies behind the protagonist's name, Tessie Hutchinson, that magnifies the allegorical force of this story. Historically, there really was a well-known New England Hutchinson— Anne Hutchinson, who, having been exiled from the Massachusetts Bay Colony in 1638 because of her religious beliefs, emigrated to Rhode Island, where she established her own church. Eventually, she and most of her family died in an Indian massacre outside of what is today New Rochelle, New York. Some might call such a woman a martyr, who was exiled and died for her beliefs. Our protagonist, however, has no strongly held beliefs, except her belief in self-survival. The name "Tessie" parodies the most famous Tess in literature, Tess Durbeyfield, the protagonist of Thomas Hardy's *Tess of the D'Ubervilles*, who in Hardy's portrait of her as the plaything of fate, dies ignominiously, since "the President of the Immortals, in Aeschylean phrase, had ended his sport with Tess." Now we must ask, Is Tessie Hutchinson in our story an ingenue, as Hardy's protagonist clearly is?

Of course not! Tessie "came hurriedly along the path to the square . . . 'Clean forgot what day it was' she said to Mrs. Delacroix . . . and they both laughed softly. . . . 'I remembered it was the twenty-seventh and came a-running.'" "Mrs. Hutchinson said, grinning, 'Wouldn't have me leave m'dishes in the sink, now, would you, Joe?'" Good-natured Tessie actually desires to come to the lottery, going so far as to run to it, although the rest of the townspeople are subdued, even nervous: the men's "jokes were quiet and they smiled rather than laughed." Mr. Summers and Mr. Adams "grinned at one another humorlessly and nervously." Young Jack Watson also appears to be nervous: "He blinked his eyes nervously and ducked his head." Later, someone in the crowd says, "'Don't be nervous, Jack.'" And not only the men are nervous, of course. "'I wish they'd hurry,' Mrs. Dunbar said to her older son. 'I wish they'd hurry.'" However, to Tessie the lottery seems to be one great lark: when her husband, Bill, is called upon to choose his family's lottery ticket, Tessie urges him, "'Get up there, Bill,'" although "by now, all through the crowd there were men holding the small folded papers in their large hands, turning them over and over nervously." What a great contrast there is, in short, between the crowd's nervousness and Tessie's nonchalance.

But when Tessie's family is chosen, she becomes a woman transformed. "Suddenly, Tessie Hutchinson shouted to Mr. Summers, 'You didn't give him time enough to take any paper he wanted. I saw you. It wasn't fair!'" Subsequently, she yells, "'There's Don and Eva [the Hutchinsons' son-in-law and daughter]. Make *them* take their chance!'" Putting aside for the moment her perfidy in singling out her married children as possible victims to increase her own chances of survival, we see that she is manifestly not the good-humored, whimsical matron whom we first saw eagerly entering the lottery. Her protests of the unfairness of the process—a thought that only now has occurred to her, since there is every likelihood of her becoming the chosen victim ("'I tell you it wasn't *fair'*")—have a distinctly hollow ring to them, and her defiant glance around the crowd, her lips pursed, as she truculently goes up to the lottery box to pick her ticket, belies her earlier easygoing demeanor. Thus, the irony behind her name has come full circle. Her final assertion ("'It isn't fair, it isn't right'") is neither the cry of an innocent victim (Tessie is definitely not Tess Durbeyfield) nor a martyr's triumphant statement (Tessie is also certainly not Anne Hutchinson). It is the peevish last complaint of a hypocrite who has been hoisted by her own petard.

—Jay A. Yarmove, "Jackson's 'The Lottery,'" *The Explicator* 52, no. 4 (Summer 1994): pp. 243–44.

[Amy A. Griffin was a literary scholar at Schreiner College. Her work has appeared in various journals including *The Explicator*. In this excerpt, Griffin discusses the role of tradition and violence in the story.]

A good harvest has always been vital to civilizations. After the fields have been prepared and the seeds sown, the farmer can only wait and hope that the proper balance of rain and sun will ensure a good harvest. From this hope springs ritual. Many ancient cultures believed that growing crops represented the life cycle, beginning with what one associates with the end—death. Seeds buried, apparently without hope of germination, represent death. But with the life forces of water and the sun, the seed grows, representing rebirth. Consequently, ancient peoples began sacrificial rituals to emulate this resurrection cycle. What began as a vegetation ritual developed into a cathartic cleansing of an entire tribe or village. By transferring one's sins to persons or animals and then sacrificing them, people believed that their sins would be eliminated, a process that has been termed the "scapegoat" archetype. In her short story "The Lottery," Shirley Jackson uses this archetype to build on man's inherent need for such ritual.

Jackson weaves seasonal and life-death cycle archetypes, which coincide with vegetation rituals, into the story. According to Carl Jung, archetypes can be considered "complexes of experience that come upon us like fate," a past collective experience represented in rituals, symbols, and motifs. The lottery takes place every year when the nature cycle peaks in midsummer, a time usually associated with cheerfulness. Mr. Summers, a jovial man who conducts the lottery ceremony, sets the tone of the event with both his name and his mannerisms. But lurking behind him, Mr. Graves quietly assists, his name hinting at a dark undertone. The piniclike atmosphere betrays the serious consequence of the lottery, for like the seed, a sacrificial person must also be buried to bring forth life. Jackson creates balance by juxtaposing Mr. Summers and Mr. Graves to share in the responsibilities of the ritual: Life brings death, and death recycles life.

At one point in the village's history, the lottery represented a grave experience, and all who participated understood the profound meaning of the tradition. But as time passed, the villagers began to take the ritual lightly. They endure it almost as automatons—"actors" anxious to return to their mundane, workaday lives. Old Man Warner, the only one who seems to recall the seriousness of the occasion, complains that Mr. Summers jokes with everybody. But why do the villagers cling to tradition when they no longer find meaning in the ritual? Jung posits that even if one does not understand the meaning, the experience provides the "individual a place and a meaning in the life of the generations." Because there has "*always* been a lottery," the villagers feel compelled to continue this horrifying tradition. They do focus, however, on its gruesome rather than its symbolic nature, for they "still remembered to use stones" even after they have "forgotten the ritual and lost the original black box." The story thus takes the stance that humanity's inclination toward violence overshadows society's need for civilized traditions.

—Amy A. Griffin, "Jackson's 'The Lottery,'" *The Explicator* 58, no. 1 (Fall 1999): pp. 44–45.

Plot Summary of
The Haunting of Hill House

The Haunting of Hill House, Shirley Jackson's eerie and highly acclaimed short novel, opens with a description of Hill House and how it has stood "holding darkness within" for eighty years. The narrative introduces John Montague, a doctor of philosophy, who has a vested interest in the supernatural. He has rented Hill House for three months in hopes that he can uncover something profound, write a book and be compensated by the royalties for his research. He has taken pains to find the ideal candidates to assist him in his research. He compiled a list consisting entirely of people who have, at least in some limited capacity, been involved in something "abnormal." Then he sent out an ambiguous, yet carefully worded letter, inviting each of these people to stay with him at Hill House.

Out of a dozen letters sent, four people reply. Dr. Montague sends an additional letter to these four, inclosing detailed directions to Hill House and citing a specific date when they can move in. Two of the four people back out at the last minute, but an extra person is added when the owner of the house insists that a representative from the family be included in the group.

Eleanor Vance is the first of the guests that is introduced. She is described as a thirty-two-year-old woman with no friends. She has spent the majority of her life taking care of her mother, whom she disliked severely. Now that her mother is dead, her sister is the only person in the world whom she hates. Eleanor is chosen by Dr. Montague because of an incident that happened when she was twelve years old—not long after her father died—when stones fell on her house for three days straight, ceasing only when Eleanor and her sister were taken out of the house.

The next guest, Theodora Vane, is a confident, spirited woman whose curiosity was sparked by the doctor's letter. She originally planned to decline the doctor's offer, but when a follow-up letter arrived just after she had a falling-out with her apartment mate, she decided that some time away might do everyone some good.

Luke Sanderson is described as a liar and a thief. He is the nephew of the owner and is sent to watch over Hill House by his aunt. Luke is set to inherit Hill House someday, and though he never considered living there he is content with the idea of joining Dr. Montague's group.

Following the sections of introduction, the narrative shifts back to Eleanor as she attempts to persuade her sister and brother-in-law to let her take the car to Hill House. Despite the fact that she paid for half of it and they likely won't need it, they are reluctant to let Eleanor drive to some foreign place. And much to her sister's displeasure, Eleanor has not told them exactly where she will be staying.

The following morning, despite her sister's protests, Eleanor sneaks out of the house and takes a taxi to the garage where they keep the car. In her nervous state, she bumps into an older woman who drops her produce on the ground. Eleanor gives her money for a cab ride home to compensate for her clumsiness.

Finally she gets on the road, reveling in her proactive decision to take the car. Before leaving town, she gets out the letter that Dr. Montague had sent and reads over the carefully detailed directions. She wants to savor every moment of her drive, as it is the first time she has done anything like this before.

As she drives, Eleanor lets her imagination run, fantasizing about the mysteries of each place she passes, and envisioning a life for herself far away from her sister. Eleanor stops for lunch in a country town where a young girl refuses to drink her milk without her "cup of stars." Eleanor relates to her and secretly hopes that she will not give in to her mother.

When she leaves the luncheonette, Eleanor becomes fearful that her journey will end too soon. She decides to stop for coffee in Hillsdale, the last town before Hill House.

Eleanor pulls into the dingy town of Hillsdale and parks outside a diner. She sits at the counter and attempts to make small talk with the waitress. She says that Hillsdale is a lovely little town and asks if they have a lot of visitors. The man sitting next to her answers that people don't come to Hillsdale, they leave it—if they're lucky.

When Eleanor arrives at Hill House, the gate is locked. She beeps the horn and a scary looking man, identified later as Dudley the caretaker, comes out. He refuses to unlock the gate at first, but after

Eleanor insists that she was invited, he lets her in. Dudley makes it clear that Hill House is not a nice place and that he always leaves before dark. Eleanor contemplates turning around, but decides that she's made this commitment, and home is not much better anyway. As she gazes around the ill-looking house, words flood into her mind: "Hill House is vile, it is diseased; get away from here at once."

Eleanor musters the strength to take her bags to the door. She knocks. Mrs. Dudley, the caretaker's wife, opens the door and leads her silently upstairs to the "blue room," where she is told to leave her things. Mrs. Dudley explains that she goes home after she sets out dinner, and never stays after dark. She adds that if anyone screamed for her in the middle of the night, she would not hear.

After Mrs. Dudley leaves the room, Eleanor tries to calm herself by reciting a line from the song that has been in her head since that morning: "Journeys end in lovers meeting." She contemplates leaving once again, but decides that since it is too late, she should get herself situated in the blue room. Eleanor unpacks her things and takes notice of the blue rug and the blue quilt and the blue walls and acknowledges that she is indeed staying in a blue room. Just when the eerie silence of the house starts to get overwhelming, she hears footsteps outside, followed by a knocking on the door. Eleanor heads quickly downstairs to greet the latest arrival.

Theodora is the next to arrive. Eleanor insists that she take the room next to hers, the green room. Mrs. Dudley states again that she sets dinner down at six, and then she leaves for the night.

Theodora and Eleanor change out of their city clothes, each choosing bright colored garments: Theodora wears a yellow shirt and Eleanor a red sweater. They head outside to explore the surroundings before dark. The two make their way through the hills that surround the house and down to a brook where they talk and laugh about their situation, planning to picnic by the brook before they leave. As they are talking, Eleanor freezes at the sound of something in the bushes. They soon realize that it's only a rabbit. Because it is getting late, they decide to head back to Hill House.

When the women return, they meet Luke Sanderson, the nephew of the owner of Hill House. They exchange some light-hearted banter and then follow him inside, where they are introduced to Dr. Montague. He beckons them into the living room and asks Luke to make martinis. When everyone has a drink, the doctor explains that he would like them each to take notes on their experience.

The house is enormous and equipped with countless small rooms that are all obscurely connected. Dr. Montague claims to have studied a map of the house, assuring the group that they will search every room the following day.

When the group gathers for dinner, they are pleasantly surprised to find the lavish display that has been left for them. While they eat, the question of why the doctor has brought them there comes up. He tries to persuade them to wait until the morning for a full explanation, but Theodora insists. Dr. Montague agrees to explain after dinner, when they can gather in the sitting room and drink brandy.

After dinner, the group gathers in the sitting room with their drinks and the doctor explains that his intentions are "scientific and exploratory." He says he's had the opportunity to come up with some theories about psychic phenomena which he hopes to test. Hill House has not had people living inside it for over twenty years. "'What it was like before then, whether its personality was molded by the people who lived here, or the things they did, or whether it was evil from its start are all questions I cannot answer," explains the doctor. Theodora asks if there was ever a scandal. The doctor replies that there was, "'A perfectly splendid scandal, with a suicide and madness and lawsuits.'"

After explaining a bit about the house, the doctor decides to speak openly about why each of them is there. He explains that Luke is the representative from the owner's family, Theodora is supposed to have an aptitude for telepathy, and Eleanor has been involved in poltergeist phenomena, citing the incident with the stone showers.

The doctor also gives the background of Hill House. It had been built eighty years ago by a man named Hugh Crain, who had planned to live there with his family. When the carriage carrying his wife overturned in the driveway, killing her before she ever stepped foot inside, he was left to raise two small daughters in the odd expanse of Hill House. Crain married two more times, his next wife dying from a fall and the final dying from consumption. It was after his final wife's death that he decided to close up the house, spend the rest of his days abroad, and send his daughters to live with a cousin of their mother's, where they remained until they were fully grown.

The doctor explains that the sisters spent a great deal of time, following the death of their father, squabbling over the rights to Hill House. Eventually it was decided that the older sister would live there because the younger sister had already married. The eldest sister lived in Hill House by herself for a number of years until she took in a girl from the village for companionship. Scandal ensued when the younger sister claimed to have given up her share of the house in exchange for specific pieces of furniture and some gold-rimmed dishes, none of which was relinquished.

The older sister eventually died of pneumonia, giving rise to more stories about her companion's neglect. The older sister's death led to a lawsuit between the younger sister and the companion. The companion was eventually awarded the house, but consistently claimed, following the death of the older sister, that she was being tormented by the younger sister and that objects were being stolen from the house. The companion eventually committed suicide, hanging herself from the turret of the tower. The house then passed legally into the hands of the Sanderson family, cousins of the former companion.

Following the doctor's story, he and Luke take up a game of chess and Eleanor sits beside Theodora to engage in conversation. The narrative dips into Eleanor's mind, exposing the depths of her self-conscious imagination. Eleanor tells Theodora about how she cared for her mother for eleven years before she finally passed away. When asked where she lives now, Eleanor tells her that she has a small place of her own which she's been decorating slowly. She describes a "cup of stars" that she used to have, pulling the description from the earlier encounter at the luncheonette, when the young girl refused to drink her milk from anything but her "cup of stars."

When the game of chess is finished, the group decides to head upstairs to bed, agreeing to walk around the house together. Eleanor asks the men what color their rooms are and Luke says that his is pink and the doctor reveals that his is yellow. Eleanor realizes how exhausted she is after the long day and is eager to lay down beneath her blue quilt.

Eleanor wakes up the next morning to find that it is after eight in the morning. It is the first good night's sleep she has had in years. When she and Theodora have bathed and dressed, they leave their rooms but can not find their way to the kitchen. Eventually the doctor locates them and claims that he had left the doors open, but they swung closed moments after they called out for assistance.

Once they all settle down for breakfast, Theodora says that she wants to see the entire house. She expresses her desire to keep all the windows and doors open so they don't have to feel their way around.

The group discusses the unique layout of the house and the incredible number of rooms. The doctor says he will explain the layout to them before they see each room individually. As he begins his explanation, Mrs. Dudley announces that it is ten o'clock and she must clear the table.

The group leaves the kitchen and starts touring through the house, propping open doors and windows, creating channels for light and air. The doctor shows them the library, positioned inside the tower. Eleanor has a reaction upon seeing it and declares that she can not go inside. The rest of the group follows the doctor into the library. They see the trap door leading to the balcony, where the woman had reportedly committed suicide. As the group stares at the tower, Theodora asks why she can't see it from her window. Dr. Montague gets noticeably excited and gestures for them to take a seat. He explains that Hugh Crain had intentionally set every angle in the house off by a small degree, to make a house that could deceive the patterns of the mind; "'Angles which you assume are the right angles you are accustomed to, and have every right to expect are true, are actually a fraction of a degree off in one direction or another.'" He explains that everything is angled subtly toward the central shaft, offering this as a rationale for why none of the doors stay open. The doctor says that the imbalance that the house promotes in the inner ear may have something to do with the cluster of mysterious events that have occurred at Hill House in the past.

The group follows Dr. Montague through a number of different rooms, making it to a drawing room near the parlor where they had had drinks the night before. They encounter an enormous statue, which they identify as a composite of the members of Hugh Crain's family. Theodora starts dancing around the statue and then incites Eleanor to run out onto the veranda with her. The two run around to the kitchen where they meet Mrs. Dudley. She exits through one of many doors and descends into the basement. After looking over

Mrs. Dudley's cooking utensils, Eleanor and Theodora decide to join Luke and the doctor outside. Eleanor walks toward the tower and starts leaning back from the veranda to get a better view. She leans further and further back until Luke finally grabs her, stressing the importance of being cautious in the imbalanced house.

After eating the soufflé that Mrs. Dudley made for lunch, the doctor suggests that an afternoon nap might be a good way for everyone to unwind. Though Eleanor could have used the sleep, she found herself following Theodora into the green room, making small conversation and watching as she paints her nails. After finishing with herself, Theodora paints Eleanor's toenails red. When Eleanor, who had been resting with her eyes closed, sees the red nail polish, she shrieks. Theodora is stunned by Eleanor's reaction and suggests that she should go home. When Eleanor calms down, they decide to find the others.

The narrative continues as Luke and the doctor discuss the house and the fact that Luke is set to inherit it. Dr. Montague tells him that he wants to take him to a particular window that has a view of the tower. He walks down the hall and enters into a large room at the end which had been the nursery. Upon crossing the threshold, he feels an unmistakable draft of cold air. The doctor reacts in a scientific manner, determined to record the exact degree of difference in temperature. Eleanor is convinced that the chill is something deliberate from the house. It is beginning to get dark so they decide to gather in the parlor for drinks.

Following dinner, the group gathers again in the parlor. Dr. Montague has a discussion with Eleanor and makes her promise that if she feels like the house is getting the best of her, she will leave. Eleanor agrees, but in her mind she feels that something wants her to stay. After Luke and the doctor finish their game of chess, the group heads off to bed.

In the middle of the night, Eleanor is woken by a noise which she initially thinks is her mother. She yells for her and her voice is heard by Theodora. Theodora tells her to come to her room and says, "in a tone of pure rationality," that something is knocking on the doors.

They huddle together in Theodora's room, listening as the noise comes closer. There is a chill that accompanies the noise. Eleanor puts her quilt around Theodora and then puts on Theodora's bathrobe. As the noise gets closer and the temperature gets colder, Eleanor runs up to the door and screams. She sits back by Theodora and they clutch each other like children until the noise is gone.

Once Theodora's room is back to normal, Luke and the doctor enter and ask if anything has happened. The two women give an ironic laugh and describe what had occurred. The doctor explains that he and Luke were lured outside by a dog. He suggests that perhaps the forces that were tormenting Eleanor and Theodora had intended to separate the men from the women.

The next morning, the group gathers downstairs for breakfast and begins discussing the events of the previous evening. Eleanor and Luke agree that despite the terrific fear they experienced, everything seemed fine now. The doctor says that no ghost has ever hurt anyone physically. "'The only damage done is by the victim to himself.'"

At ten o'clock, Mrs. Dudley demands that the table be vacated. The group gathers in the parlor and the doctor says that he wants more coffee. He asks Luke if he will request it from Mrs. Dudley. Luke leaves and comes back moments later, his face deathly pale. He gestures for the group to follow him into the hall. He points to the wall where a message has been written in chalk. The doctor shines his flashlight on it. The message reads "HELP ELEANOR COME HOME."

Eleanor gets noticeably upset and demands that the message be erased. She is helped into the parlor where she worries aloud about the message and the implications of being singled out. As Eleanor gets increasingly worked up, she and Theodora get into an argument. Eventually they apologize to one another, though Eleanor's thoughts, chronicled by the narrative, are paranoid and hyper.

After the incident with the chalk, things seem to calm down. The doctor and Luke try to measure the cold area outside the nursery and attempt to record the difference in temperature. But despite the undeniable degree of difference, the thermometer refuses to acknowledge any change. Dr. Montague informs the group that the Saturday coming up, his wife will be joining them in Hill House. The group remarks that they hope she won't be disappointed as nothing too drastic has happened in a little while.

Following lunch, Eleanor and Theodora head upstairs to relax in their respective rooms. As Eleanor enters into the blue room she hears Theodora scream. Eleanor sprints next door to find another message scrawled out in blood. Theodora accuses Eleanor of writing the message. Then she breaks down and Eleanor is forced to alert the doctor and Luke. When they come to Theo's room, they read the message: "HELP ELEANOR COME HOME ELEANOR"

Despite being identified in the message, Eleanor keeps her composure and suggests that Theodora be taken into her room. The doctor commends Eleanor for keeping her head, but inside, Eleanor is filling up with a curious loathing for Theodora. She goes into her room and sees Theodora resting on her bed, staining her sheets with the blood on her hands. Eleanor feels an unmistakable feeling of hatred for her, but does her best to keep it inside. Luke brings in a bed and comments that Theodora and Eleanor will now be sharing clothes and a room.

Later that evening, the group convenes in the parlor for drinks. Theodora is dressed in Eleanor's red sweater. Eleanor is unreasonably upset, though she does her best to conceal her feelings. Following some casual conversation, Eleanor reveals that she was afraid earlier in the afternoon, even though she didn't show it. She goes on to say how frightening it is to see her name written on the wall. This leads her into a monologue about selfhood, ending with the statement "'if I could only surrender . . .'" The entire group reacts to her use of the word "surrender" and implores her to finish her brandy and try not to be the center of attention.

Theodora and Eleanor settle down to sleep, their beds positioned side by side. When the chill starts, they clutch hands and brave the eerie cackling and groaning. As the conditions worsen, Eleanor realizes that it is dark in the room, though she remembers leaving the lights on. She tries to ask why it is dark, but her mouth won't work. A sobbing child can be heard from some distant place in the house. Eleanor gets increasingly frightened and upset. She clutches Theodora's hand with both of her own, feeling the slender bones in Theo's fingers. The noises intensify. Unable to stand it any longer, Eleanor cries out "'STOP IT'" only to find that the lights are on and Theodora is sitting up in her bed. Eleanor jumps onto the floor and runs into the corner of the room. As she shakes from fear she asks aloud "'God God—whose hand was I holding?'"

The next day, Eleanor sits outside with Luke and they have a strained and awkward discussion. He tells her that he never had a mother and he realizes how much he has missed. He reminds her how lucky she was to have had a mother.

The narrative resumes later in the day, as Luke is showing the doctor and the rest of the group the enormous scrap book that he found. The book was put together by Hugh Crain and is dedicated to his daughters. Inside there are pictures and passages about the tortures of hell and the splendors of heaven. There is a list of the seven deadly sins and pictures and descriptions to accompany each sin. And the final inscription is signed in Hugh Crain's own blood.

The action resumes in the parlor as Luke and the doctor play chess and Theodora and Eleanor sit together beside the fire. Theodora mocks Eleanor for having spent time alone with Luke. Eleanor suffers silently through Theodora's ridicule before she excuses herself and walks outside, into the dark evening air. Theodora follows her and the two walk together down a hillside path. Before long, they are struck by how dark the path has become. They walk swiftly along the winding path, afraid to turn around or stop. Eleanor imagines she sees a picnic up ahead, with children and tables. Then Theodora screams and the two run for the house. When they arrive, the doctor and Luke claim to have been searching for them for hours. Eleanor mentions the picnic and Theodora laughs maniacally.

The following evening, Mrs. Montague, the doctor's wife, arrives at Hill House with Arthur Parker, a school headmaster and friend. Mrs. Montague is a demanding woman who asks to be placed in the most haunted room. Her husband suggests the nursery, telling her of the cold draft that guards the entrance. Mrs. Montague expresses disdain at how frightened her husband and his guests appear.

The doctor shows his wife and Arthur to the dining room where dinner had been left for them. Mrs. Montague immediately acknowledges the surprising quality of Mrs. Dudley's food. She informs her husband that she and Arthur will have to leave on Monday afternoon as Arthur has classes to teach.

After dinner, Mrs. Montague tells of her plans to have a session with planchette. Arthur explains that planchette "'is a device similar to the Ouija board,'" used to communicate with the spirits.

The narrative resumes after Arthur and Mrs. Montague return from their spiritual session. Mrs. Montague tells her husband, who is skeptical of planchette's powers, that a nun may have been walled up alive inside the confines of Hill House. The doctor is dismissive of her claims until she reveals that they have a message about one of the members of the group. She says that they communicated with a spirit who called herself Eleanor. The spirit said repeatedly that she wanted to go home. When Arthur and the doctor's wife asked why she wanted to go home, the spirit answered "mother."

Arthur decides that he will spend the night in the small room next to the nursery. He is equipped with a revolver, a flashlight, and a whistle. Mrs. Montague says that he'll be patrolling the upstairs every hour, starting at midnight. After Mrs. Montague and Arthur retire to their rooms, the rest of the group gathers in the doctor's room to discuss their latest arrivals.

Soon after the group is together, the door to the doctor's room is slammed shut and the pounding noise and extreme cold, experienced in recent nights, returns in force. Eleanor and Theodora huddle tightly together beneath a blanket. Eleanor feels like the noise is coming from inside her own head. She senses that she is "disappearing inch by inch into this house."

As the rattling intensifies, Eleanor slips further into a realm of her own, feeling as much like an observer as a participant. Finally she hears herself relent to the voices in her head, saying aloud "'I'll come.'" Her acquiescence seems to quiet the rattling house. Then she wakes, as if from a dream, in the doctor's room. The group is laughing from relief. Eleanor is noticeably confused. Theodora offers to wash her up and bring her to their room.

The following morning at breakfast, Arthur and Mrs. Montague remark on the lack of activity during the past evening. Following the morning meal, when Eleanor and Theodora are writing their notes, Eleanor reveals her plan to come home with Theodora after their stay in Hill House. Theodora makes it clear that she would not be welcome to do that. Luke meets up with Eleanor and Theodora and decides to join them on a walk to the brook. Theodora tells Luke of Eleanor's odd plan. Eleanor stops speaking. While Luke talks with Theodora about Eleanor's state of mind, he recites the exact line which runs frequently through Eleanor's head: "Journeys end in lovers meeting."

Eleanor breaks her silence by announcing that she is to blame for her mother's death. She claims that her mother had knocked on her wall, desperate for her medication, but she never woke up. Luke and Theodora dismiss her claim as silly and continue to talk on their own. As they walk along the path, the narrative dips into Eleanor's head. She is convinced that she will be going home with Theodora after Hill House, and that Theo is excited about it. She imagines that she will help out in Theodora's shop. When Eleanor arrives at the brook, she realizes that she is alone. Then she hears footsteps and her name being called both inside and outside her head. She flees up the path, and finds Theodora and Luke sitting against a tree. They claim to have wanted to rest in the shade.

After lunch, Theodora and Luke walk outside. Eleanor follows them, hiding behind the summerhouse to listen to their conversation. Luke offers to sing a song called "The Grattan Murders" to Theodora. The lyrics detail (in rhyme) how each member of the Grattan family got killed. When Luke is finished singing, they speak for a moment about the doctor's book, and what will be included.

Following dinner that evening, Eleanor hears the words of a song in her head and relishes in the joy that she is the only one who can hear it. The rest of the room is occupied with the sound of Mrs. Montague, who is upset that planchette is not giving her anything, blaming the silence on the skepticism of her husband.

That night, driven by the forces within her, Eleanor decides to leave her room and visit the library. When she gets to the bottom of the stairs, she hears a voice calling to her from the upstairs hallway. She suspects it's her mother and goes upstairs to find her. When she gets to the landing, she searches for the voice. She walks to the nursery door and discovers that the cold chill is no longer there. She knocks on the door and Mrs. Montague, woken by the noise, asks who (or what) is there. Realizing that no one would open their door at this hour, she starts running up and down the hall, banging on everyone's door, recreating the ruckus that had occurred on previous nights.

Eleanor is startled when she hears Theodora calling out her name. Realizing that someone might open their door to search for her, she decides to descend the stairs again. She flees into the parlor and listens as the group searches for her. Eleanor runs playfully around the lower level, reveling in the fun of eluding her companions. When she hears Luke's voice behind her, she escapes into the library. She acknowledges that it is not as cold and dreary as she had expected. She decides to ascend the winding, iron stairway, climbing toward the top of the tower.

When she gets to the narrow platform at the top of the stairway, she is spotted by the group. They call out to her, imploring her to remain still. After pounding on the trapdoor, pleading with it to open, she sees Luke climbing after her. Mrs. Montague insists that the platform can not hold them both. Finally Luke makes it to the top and guides Eleanor down to the ground.

The following morning, there is an awkward silence at the breakfast table. Eleanor tries to deny that anything is different. But after breakfast, the doctor tells her that Luke will be bringing her car around and Theodora will be packing up her clothes. Eleanor laughs and reminds them that Theodora will need her clothes. Mrs. Montague informs her that she inspected Theodora's room and her clothes are perfectly fine. Eleanor protests, claiming that it would be impossible for her to leave. The doctor, slightly frustrated, tells her that she has no choice.

The group lines up outside to bid Eleanor farewell. The doctor recites the directions to her as she gazes over the landscape of Hill House. Eleanor apologizes to the doctor. Luke and Dr. Montague take her to her car door and guide her inside. The doctor insists that she go, suggesting that she will forget all about Hill House.

After saying goodbye, Eleanor releases the brake and lets the car move slowly down the drive. She mocks the doctor who had insisted that she go. She laughs and thinks that the house is not as easy to deceive as the group. The house doesn't want her to leave, she thinks. So in an act that she perceives as "quick cleverness," she slams the accelerator to the floor and steers directly toward the large oak tree at the curve of the driveway. The instant before she crashes into the tree she thinks "Why am I doing this? Why am I doing this? Why don't they stop me?"

Following Eleanor's death, the entire group leaves Hill House. Theodora is accepted graciously back by her companion, Luke heads off to Paris to live indefinitely, and Dr. Montague retires from scholarly life, his initial essay about his experience in Hill House a failure. The final words of the novel are devoted toward the empty state of Hill House, and how anything that walks within, walks alone. ✿

List of Characters in
The Haunting of Hill House

Eleanor Vance is the highly imaginative, yet severely self-conscious central character. She had been taking care of her difficult, ailing mother before her death. She lived briefly with her sister and her brother-in-law before responding to Dr. Montague's letter and driving to Hill House. She becomes the focus of Hill House's attention. Her name appears in cryptic messages that manifest periodically throughout the novel. She gradually loses her grip on reality and is asked to leave by the doctor. As she is pulling out of the driveway, she veers intentionally into the oak tree and kills herself.

Dr. John Montague instigates the Hill House gathering in an effort to acquire data on psychic phenomena and write a book. He has studied the lay-out of Hill House and does his best to explain the unusual occurrences scientifically. When his wife shows up, he loses some of his control over the proceedings. He insists that Eleanor leave Hill House after it is clear that she has lost her grip on reality.

Theodora Vane decides to come to Hill House after having a falling-out with her apartment mate. She is an attractive, yet jealous, person who contributes to Eleanor's mental disintegration.

Luke Sanderson is the nephew of the owner of Hill House. His aunt insists that he stay with Dr. Montague's group as a representative of her estate. He helps Eleanor down from the tower after she had climbed to the top—the action that forced the doctor to insist that she leave.

Mrs. Dudley is the cook and caretaker of Hill House. She is a cold woman, with rigid regulations, but a surprisingly talented cook.

Mr. Dudley is the husband of Mrs. Dudley. He reluctantly lets everyone inside the gate upon their arrival.

Mrs. Montague is the demanding wife of Dr. Montague. She arrives after the group had been in Hill House for a week. She discloses a message about Eleanor that planchette, her device for communicating with the spirits, relays to her.

Arthur Parker is the headmaster of a school. He drives Mrs. Montague to Hill House and joins her in the process of communicating with planchette. ❀

Critical Views on
The Haunting of Hill House

MAXWELL GEISMAR ON THE AUTHOR'S WRITING SKILL

[Maxwell Geismar was a scholar and literary critic who published many articles, reviews, and critical volumes. He was the author of *American Moderns*, a survey of contemporary fiction. In this excerpt, Geismar speaks on how Jackson is better at capturing the supernatural world than she is the normal one.]

If Miss Jackson is proficient in describing the alarums and excursions of human pathology, she is correspondingly weak on the "normal" world of human relations, or even of ordinary social gossip. The two women in the story, Eleanor and Theodora, engage in a curious kind of infantile Lesbian affection that is meant to be sophisticated, but is usually embarrassing. There is too much of this whimsy in the earlier parts of the novel; eventually it turns out that both women have an eye on Luke, and that their real relation is one of love-hate. While all this goes on, the doctor lectures us intermittently on the role played by haunted houses in the annals of magic.

It is only when the monster at Hill House strikes at last (and how!) that Miss Jackson's pen becomes charmed, or rather demonic, and the supernatural activity is really chilling. Who or what is it that closes every door in this "masterpiece of architectural misdirection"; that has the smell of putrefaction, the cold breath of death; that writes on the wall, pounds at the doors, whimpers and snickers, and leaves its tracks in a substance indistinguishable from blood? Our suspicion falls in turn upon each member of the little group, and then in particular upon one of the girls, Eleanor, who has been selected, it appears, as the special "victim" of the monster.

In fairness to Miss Jackson's readers, I can say no more than this—though my own conviction is that the author is not altogether fair with us. After the crime tales of a William Roughead, or the mystery tales of Henry James himself, we are bound to expect a "rationale" of even the supernatural. Miss Jackson never deigns to offer this to us. She is concerned only with the effect of a terrifying atmosphere—

which she calls "reality"—upon a mind already preoccupied with horrors. But in this rather restricted and peculiar medium Shirley Jackson is, I must say, very eloquent.

—Maxwell Geismar, "*The Haunting of Hill House*, by Shirley Jackson," *Saturday Review* (31 October 1959): pp. 19, 31.

⊗

LENEMAJA FRIEDMAN ON THE BACKGROUND OF THE STORY

[Lenemaja Friedman is a professor of English Literature at Columbus College. She has published short stories and reviewed several books for *Choice* magazine. In this excerpt, Friedman discusses Jackson's inspiration for writing the novel.]

The inspiration to write a ghost story came to Miss Jackson, according to her account in the article "Experience and Fiction," as she was reading a book about a group of nineteenth-century psychic researchers who rented a haunted house in order to study it and record their impressions of what they had seen and heard for the purpose of presenting a treatise to the Society for Psychic Research. As she recalls: "They thought that they were being terribly scientific and proving all kinds of things, and yet the story that kept coming through their dry reports was not at all the story of a haunted house, it was the story of several earnest, I believe misguided, certainly determined people, with their differing motivations and backgrounds." The story so excited her that she could hardly wait to create her own haunted house and her own people to study it.

Shortly thereafter, she states, on a trip to New York, she saw at the 125th Street station, a grotesque house—one so evil-looking, one that made such a somber impression, that she had nightmares about it long afterward. In response to her curiosity, a New York friend investigated and found that the house, intact from the front, was merely a shell since a fire had gutted the structure, leaving only the frame of the remaining walls. In the meantime, she was searching newspapers, magazines, and books for pictures of suitably haunted-looking houses; and she at last discovered a magazine picture of a house that seemed just right. It looked very much like the hideous building she had seen in New York: ". . . it had the same air of disease and decay, and if ever a house looked like a candidate for a ghost, it was this one." The picture identified the house as being in a California town; consequently, hoping her mother in California might be able to acquire some information about the house, she wrote asking for help. As it happened, her mother was not only familiar with the house but provided the startling information that Miss Jackson's great-grandfather had built it. Apparently, it had stood vacant and deserted for many years until, it was believed, a group of townspeople burned it down. She had been surprised that there were still pictures of the house in circulation.

While seeking the proper house, Miss Jackson did research about ghosts. As she says, she had always been interested in witchcraft and superstition, but she knew little about spirits. Her information came from personal inquiry and the reading of books, especially true ghost stories. No one that she contacted had ever seen a ghost, but most people had the uneasy suspicion that, at some undisclosed time, they just might run into one. After the house had been selected and with the psychic research well under way, the writing went smoothly. Finally, the novel was finished; published in 1959 by the Viking Press, it went through several printings and many foreign editions; it was hailed by critics as one of the best spine-chillers in years.

—Lenemaja Friedman, *Shirley Jackson* (Boston: Twayne Publishers, 1975): pp. 121–22.

☙

JOHN G. PARKS ON THE STORY'S CHARACTERS

[John G. Parks is a professor of English at Miami University in Ohio. He has published articles and reviews in *Critique, Studies in Short Fiction,* and *Modern Fiction Studies.* In this excerpt, Parks discusses the presence of the House in the story, particularly within the central character, Eleanor Vance.]

While a setting for what begins as a mad masquerade party in *The Sundial*, the gothic house in a real sense is the chief character of *The Haunting of Hill House* (1959), Jackson's fifth and probably most popular novel. Its presence is felt on nearly every page. The house is over eighty years old and carries the unsavory reputation of death, madness, revenge, and suicide. It is marked by "clashing disharmony," everything off center, made entirely at "wrong angles," all the small aberrations adding up to a rather large distortion. Its basic structure is laid out in concentric circles, with rooms surrounded by other rooms—a "mother house." It is a fitting metaphor for madness, for the irrational, for an illogic that perversely coheres. In classic gothic fiction, as Devendra P. Varma reminds us, "the element of terror is inseparably associated with the Gothic castle, which is an image of power, dark, isolated, and impenetrable." To the Romantic movement and in gothic fiction "the castle stands as a central image of the lonely personality." It is this house which welcomes home the utterly guilt-ridden, lonely, and loveless protagonist, Eleanor Vance, who surrenders willingly to its dark embraces, her own fragile self dissolving and fusing with the substance of Hill House.

Eleanor Vance, another of Jackson's violated women, is brought to Hill House as part of a scientific experiment into psychic phenomena. She is so fragile and vulnerable that her survival is questionable from the beginning. Her chief foil, reminiscent of Dr. Wright of *The Bird's Nest*, is Dr. Montague, a pompous academic representing scientific rationalism and logic. He is little more than an intellectual voyeur, knowing very much, but really understanding very little, especially when it comes to the mysteries of the human personality and the human heart. Terror and fear, the fatuous doctor believes, can be explained and controlled in terms of logic and will: "'Fear . . . is the relinquishment of logic, the *willing* relinquishment of reasonable patterns. We yield to it or we fight it, but we cannot meet it half way.'" This militant rationalist shows little compassion for Eleanor's loss of sanity and banishes her from the house to protect his so-called experiment.

The character Theodora is another of Jackson's "dark ladies," recalling the figure of Tony in *Hangsaman*. She is the opposite of Eleanor. She is secular and much experienced, exotic and exciting, representing, in part, what Eleanor might have been if her life had not been so restricted and inhibited. At times Theodora's ministrations to Eleanor verge on the lesbian. At other times she ridicules Eleanor, and when Eleanor desperately reaches out for help, Theodora turns away abandoning her to her lonely dissolution. If Theodora functions partly as Eleanor's *Doppelgänger,* she does so in the sense of representing what Barbara Hill Rigney refers to as "the tragedy of one's own fragmentation and alienation from the self."

There is no place in the world for Eleanor. Unlike the Apollonian Dr. Montague, the Dionysian and cynical Theodora, Eleanor has no resources to call upon for survival. Her loneliness and schizophrenia find a welcome in the chaos of Hill House. If Eleanor is abandoned to suicide, the house remains unconquerable, eluding the vain assaults of rationality and pointing to the mysterious and incomprehensible.

—John G. Parks, "Chambers of Yearning: Shirley Jackson's Use of the Gothic," *Twentieth Century Literature* 30, no. 1 (Spring 1984): pp. 24–26.

☙

MARY KITTREDGE ON HILL HOUSE'S EVIL FORCE

[Mary Kittredge is the former editor of *Empire* magazine. Her fiction has appeared in *Twilight Zone* and *Isaac Asimov's Science Fiction Magazine.* In this excerpt, Kittredge discusses the personality of evil in the story.]

The Sundial offers no psychological explanations of the numerous supernatural events that occur in it, and in this respect represents a shift in Shirley Jackson's treatment of the subject. In previous books, weird happenings grew out of weird psyches; here, however, they occur independently and are apparently meant to be taken at face value; the snake that appears in the house, for example, is no ordinary snake, but it is quite real and not a figment of madness or imagination.

In *The Haunting of Hill House,* Jackson takes this shift a step further, giving the evil force not just reality, but personality and purpose. As in *The Sundial,* the supernatural in *Haunting* is neither product nor facet of the main character's mind; it is outside her, and independently real. It does not occupy her; rather, it lures and seduces her away from the pains and problems of the real world into a ghostly existence as another haunting spirit. In *Haunting,* the evil is developed to the point of winning the conflict; there is no happy ending for the heroine, because her character is too weak for the battle. She does not choose madness, but is overwhelmed by it.

In *Haunting,* the most "supernatural" of her full-length works, Shirley Jackson for the first time gives the devil his due. She puts her damsel into mortal distress and leaves her there, completely unrescued. The potential for disaster is fully explored; the evil force is developed into a completely independent and alien entity, and is shown to be a power that can triumph.

In this bleak and chilling twist on the house-with-the-terrible-secret gothic, the heroine dies. While she is the most psychically sensitive of the guests at Hill House, she is also the most susceptible to the forces there. Her personality is weak and poorly integrated; her "magic," the magic of life, is not sufficiently developed to survive a confrontation with the magic of death. With few satisfactions of her own, she has throughout her peril been wishing to merge herself with someone else, so that she will not have to make a life for herself. She harbors also the expectant fantasy that she will be rescued.

But the rescuing prince never appears. Unable to rescue herself, she succumbs to the power of the house, which chillingly grants her desire and makes her life part of its own.

—Mary Kittredge, "The Other Side of Magic: A Few Remarks About Shirley Jackson," in *Discovering Modern Horror Fiction,* ed. Darrell Schweitzer (Mercer Island, Wash.: Starmont House, 1985): p. 8.

⊛

CAROL CLEVELAND ON ELEANOR VANCE

[Carol Cleveland is a contributor to *Twentieth Century Crime and Mystery Writers.* She works as an adjunct professor and a freelance writer. In this excerpt, Cleveland speaks on the emotional state of the central character in the story, and Jackson's ability to translate this state into various literary genres.]

In *The Haunting of Hill House, The Bird's Nest* and *Hangsaman,* Jackson gives the reader portraits of three young women in various degrees of mental and emotional disarray, which has been caused or exacerbated by their families. Eleanor Vance, Natalie Waite and Elizabeth Richmond are all entering on the same crucial phase of their growth—the last step into the adult world as independent people. All find themselves coming seriously apart when confronted with this task.

Jackson had a strong penchant for mixing genres and reversing conventional expectations. In *The Haunting of Hill House,* she takes a tired formula from the gothic romance and turns it inside out to tell a genuine ghost story with strong roots in psychological realism. The classic gothic formula brings a vulnerable young girl to an isolated mansion with a reputation for ghosts, exposes her to a few weird happenings to heighten the suspense, then explains the "supernatural" away by a perfectly human, if evil, plot and leaves the heroine in the strong arms of the hero. In *House,* the heroine is exceedingly vulnerable, the weird happenings quite real, the house really haunted.

Eleanor Vance, as unmarried daughters have been expected to do, has spent her youth taking care of a bedridden mother. This has "left her with some proficiency as a nurse and an inability to face strong sunlight without blinking." Eleanor's sister and brother-in-law have rewarded her for this long and faithful service with a cot in their daughter's bedroom and half interest in a car. The "strong sunlight" that Eleanor blinks at is normal life; she is incapable of relaxed adult conversation; she is desperate for an independent, satisfying life, and she is almost completely without the means of achieving it. She has so little experience that she will take anything offered.

What fate offers is Hill House, which is mad. She is summoned by Dr. John Montague to be part of a ghost-hunting house party. She has been chosen because of a poltergeist incident dating from her adolescence. Jackson assumes that poltergeist phenomena happen, that they are the result of repressed emotion and that Eleanor is author and victim of the increasingly frightening events that follow the installation of the party of four at Hill House. Jackson also assumes that houses and other locales can be the centers of evil associations—wells of misery and agony waiting for suitably tenuous human beings to drink from them. What Eleanor needs in order to have any hope of survival is a place to belong, where she is welcome for herself, not suffered as a duty. Hill House welcomes her. She is exactly the personality it has been waiting for.

—Carol Cleveland, "Shirley Jackson" in *And Then There Were Nine . . . More Women of Mystery,* ed. Jane S. Bakerman (Bowling Green, Ohio: Bowling Green State University Popular Press, 1985): pp. 202–3.

⊗

Lynette Carpenter on Shirley Jackson's Female Characters

[Lynette Carpenter is Director of Women's Studies and Professor of English at the University of Cincinnati. She is the co-editor of the critical collection *Haunting the House of Fiction: Feminist Perspectives on Women's Ghost Stories.* In this excerpt, Carpenter discusses Jackson's portrayal of women in stories such as *The Haunting of Hill House.*]

If, as Wilt argues, matriarchal comics elect the safest way to express the frustrations of the female role in a sexist society, Jackson's uniqueness lies in her use of other more dangerous means as well. In fiction, she writes most often about women. The typical Jackson protagonist is a lonely young woman struggling toward maturity. She is a social misfit, not beautiful enough, charming enough, or articulate enough to get along well with other people, too introverted and awkward. In short, she does not fit any of the feminine stereotypes available to her. She is Harriet Merriam in *The Road Through the Wall* (1948), an overweight teenager who thinks to herself, "You'll always be fat, . . . never pretty, never charming, never dainty," and who may have been the one to murder pink and white, doll-like Caroline Desmond because the little girl was everything Harriet was not. She is Natalie Waite in *Hangsaman* (1951), whose feelings of isolation and alienation during her first few months away at college generate a fantasy other, an imaginary friend. She is Elizabeth Richmond in *The Bird's Nest* (1954), whose adolescent confusion about her mother and her mother's lover splits her at last into a tangle of discrete personalities. She is Eleanor Vance in *The Haunting of Hill House* (1959), whose feelings of rejection and social displacement ultimately lead her to suicide. She is Mary Katherine

Blackwood in *We Have Always Lived in the Castle* (1962), who lives with her sister in a state of siege, barricaded against a town's hostility. She is Mrs. Angela Motorman in *Come Along With Me* (unfinished, 1965), whose world has always been peopled by creatures no one else can see. She is even Aunt Fanny in *The Sundial* (1958), whose life of uselessness as a maiden aunt is vindicated by a vision of doomsday.

These women are all victims, and several are clearly victimized by men. Elizabeth Richmond's split personality in *The Bird's Nest* is a result of her mother's neglect, but also of sexual exploitation by her mother's lover. Patriarchs, however, are often the villains. Natalie Waite's father in *Hangsaman* attempts to continue his proprietary control of her intellectual development even after she has gone off to college, just as Aunt Fanny's father presides over her life from beyond the grave by sending her visions of Armageddon. Mary Katherine Blackwood of *We Have Always Lived in the Castle* is the strongest of Jackson's heroines: she retaliates against her tyrannical father by poisoning him, along with most of the rest of her family. Patriarchy is not beside the point in this novel; Mary Katherine's brother, heir to Blackwood male power, gets the most arsenic. The climax of the novel occurs when a male cousin, supported by the men of the town, attempts to assume her father's role as family head and dictator.

Equally interesting to the feminist critic should be Jackson's portrayal of women's relationships to other women, beginning with her portrayal of adolescent friendships in *The Road Through the Wall*. For most of the girls on Pepper Street, allegiances are drawn by intimidation; the most outspoken and audacious girls attract followers, until a tacitly understood hierarchy exists. Overweight Harriet Merriam, however, manages to develop a close friendship with the Jewish outcast Marilyn Perlman, until Mrs. Merriam intervenes. Without someone to share her ostracism, Harriet falls victim to despair. In *The Haunting of Hill House*, the lonely Eleanor Vance becomes infatuated with the beautiful Theodora when both are invited to a haunted house by a psychic investigator. The appearance of a young man introduces rivalry, tension, and cruelty into the relationship, as Eleanor struggles to maintain her favored status with Theodora. Eleanor kills herself when she is sent away and perceives that she is again to be excluded.

—Lynette Carpenter, "Domestic Comedy, Black Comedy, and Real Life: Shirley Jackson, A Woman Writer," in *Faith of a (Woman) Writer*, edited by Alice Kessler-Harris and William McBrien (New York: Greenwood Press, 1988): pp. 145–46.

@

JUDY OPPENHEIMER ON WRITING THE STORY

[Judy Oppenheimer has been a reporter at *The Washington Post*, movie critic at the *Philadelphia Daily News*, and associate editor of the *Montgomery Sentinel*. Her writing has appeared in *Ms.*, the *Village Voice*, and the *Manchester Guardian*. In this excerpt, Oppenheimer discusses the process involved in writing the story and the acclaim received once the novel was released.]

The result, *The Haunting of Hill House*, has been called by no less an authority than Stephen King one of the greatest horror novels of all time. King, in fact, dedicated one of his books, *Firestarter*, "to Shirley Jackson, who never had to raise her voice." *Hill House* is eerie, subtle, infinitely chilling. "I have always loved to use fear," she said—and she rarely used it better.

During her research, she had asked a number of people what they thought of ghosts, and discovered there was "one common factor—most people have never seen a ghost, and never want or expect to, but almost everyone will admit that sometimes they have a sneaking feeling that they just possibly could meet a ghost if they weren't careful—if they were to turn a corner too suddenly, perhaps, or open their eyes too soon when they wake up at night, or go into a dark room without hesitating first." And it was this feeling of fearful half-expectancy that Shirley played on. The effects in *Hill House* are offstage, indirect, unexplained, elusive; not just the characters but the readers too are not sure what they have or have not actually experienced. Quite a feat to pull off in cold print.

The story is about a group of people brought together by a psychic researcher to investigate a particular house; all are supposed to have some sensitivity to supernatural forces. The dark energies of what Shirley called "Hill House, not sane" are aroused by the main character, Eleanor, an odd, lonely girl who feels her first sense of happiness and pleasure when at the house. Whether the ghostly effects are caused by the house itself or by the unconscious workings of Eleanor's mind or by some strange combination of the two is never known. (As Barry says, What difference would it make?) But at the house, Eleanor experiences a sense of belonging for the first time, even amid the horror, and she refuses to give up what is hers. When forced to leave, she smashes her car into a tree, killing herself, triumphantly. For it is not a defeat, far from it—in the moment she makes her decision to merge with the dark powers, Eleanor is more blazingly alive than she has ever been in her life.

> —Judy Oppenheimer, *Private Demons: The Life of Shirley Jackson* (New York: Fawcett Columbine, 1988): pp. 226–27.

(ᘖ)

JUDIE NEWMAN ON THE MOTHER-DAUGHTER RELATIONSHIP IN THE STORY

[Judie Newman has taught English Literature at the University of Newcastle. She is the author of *Saul Bellow and History, John Updike,* and *Nadine Gordimer.* In this excerpt, Newman discusses the significance of the mother-daughter relationship in the story.]

An exploration of *The Haunting of Hill House* in the light of feminist psychoanalytic theory reveals that the source of both the pleasures and the terrors of the text springs from the dynamics of the mother-daughter relation with its attendant motifs of psychic annihilation, reabsorption by the mother, vexed individuation, dissolution of individual ego boundaries, terror of separation and the attempted reproduction of the symbiotic bond through close female friendship. Eleanor Vance, the central protagonist, is mother-dominated. On her father's death the adolescent Eleanor was associated with an outbreak of poltergeist activity, in which her family home was repeatedly showered with stones. The event invites comparison with 'The Lottery,' in which the victim of the stoning, Tessie Hutchinson, is not only a mother, but a mother who sees her daughter as so much an extension of herself that she attempts to improve her own chances of survival by involving Eva in the fatal draw. Eleanor clearly resented her recently dead mother, whom she nursed for eleven years: 'the only person in the world she genuinely hated, now that her mother was dead, was her sister.' Initially her excursion to Hill House to participate in Dr. Montague's study of psychic phenomena appears as an opportunity for psychological liberation, the first steps towards autonomy. The trip begins with a small act of assertion against the mother-image. When Eleanor's sister refuses to allow her to use their shared car ('I am sure Mother would have agreed with me, Eleanor'), Eleanor reacts by simply stealing it, in the process knocking over an angry old woman who is clearly associated with the 'cross old lady' whom she had nursed for so long. Once *en route* Eleanor is haunted by the refrain 'Journeys end in lovers meeting,' suggesting (as the *carpe diem* theme of the song confirms) that Eleanor's goal is the realisation of heterosexual desires.

Eleanor's fantasies on the journey, however, imply that her primary emotional relation remains with her mother. In imagination she dreams up several 'homes,' based on houses on her route. In the first, 'a little dainty old lady took care of me,' bringing trays of tea and wine 'for my health's sake.' The fantasy reveals just how much Eleanor herself wishes to be mothered. In the preceding period, as nurse to a sick mother, Eleanor may be said to have 'mothered' her own mother, losing her youth in the process. A second fantasy centres upon a hollow square of poisonous oleanders, which seem to Eleanor to be 'guarding something.' Since the oleanders enclose only an empty centre, Eleanor promptly supplies a mother to occupy it, constructing an enthralling fairy world in which 'the queen waits, weeping, for the princess to return.' Though she swiftly revises this daydream of mother-daughter reunion, into a more conventional fantasy of courtship by a handsome prince, she remains much preoccupied with images of protected spaces and magic enclosures, of a home in which *she* could be mothered and greeted as a long-lost child. A subsequent incident reinforces this impression. Pausing for lunch, Eleanor observes a little girl who refuses to drink her milk because it is not in the familiar cup, patterned with stars, which she uses at home. Despite material persuasion, the child resists, forcing her mother to yield. The small tableau emphasises both the child's potential independence and resistance to the mother, and the attractions of the familiar home world, here associated with mother's milk and starry containment. Eleanor emphathises with the little girl's narcissistic desires: 'insist on your cup of stars; once they have trapped you into being like everyone else you will never see your cup of stars again.' Eleanor's final fantasy home, a cottage hidden behind oleanders, 'buried in a garden,' is entirely secluded from the world. Taken together, her fantasies suggest her ambivalent individuation and the lure of a magic mother-world. They form a striking contrast to the reality of Hillsdale, a tangled mess of dirty houses and crooked streets. For all its ugliness, however, Eleanor deliberately delays there over coffee. Despite her reiterated refrain 'In delay there lies no plenty,' Eleanor is not quite so eager to reach her goal and realise her desires as she thinks. Another scene of enforced delay, negotiating with a surly caretaker at the gates of Hill House, further retards her progress. The emphasis here on locked gates, guards against entry, a tortuous access road, and the general difficulty in locating the house reinforces the impression of its desirability as *heimlich*, secret, a home kept away from the eyes of others.

—Judie Newman, "Shirley Jackson and the Reproduction of Mothering: *The Haunting of Hill House*," in *American Horror Fiction: From Brockden Brown to Stephen King*, ed. Brian Docherty (New York: St. Martin's Press, 1990): pp. 122–24.

TRICIA LOOTENS ON SEXUALITY IN THE STORY

[Tricia Lootens is a professor of English at the University of Georgia. She is a regular contributor to the feminist newspaper *off our backs*. In this excerpt, Lootens discusses the destructive role of sexuality in the story.]

When Theodora paints Eleanor's toenails red in a scene added to the final draft, the gesture is both seductive and aggressive. She mockingly validates Eleanor's earlier fantasy of being a "famous courtesan," but she also says, "By the time I'm through with you, you will be a different person; I dislike being with women of no color."

This scene and Hill House's response to it are roughly framed by two others. In the first, in a rare moment of pleasure in her own separate identity, Eleanor finds herself "unexpectedly admiring her own [unpainted] feet." That same evening, Theodora tells Eleanor she is attractive and touches her hand. Eleanor, who tells herself she hates to be touched, is suddenly afraid she herself is not "clean": "Her fingernails *were* dirty, and her hand was badly shaped," she thinks, "and people made jokes about love because sometimes it was funny." After the toenail painting and its sequel, the guests discover a ghastly book of precepts for one of the original daughters of Hill House, compiled by the self-proclaimed "author of [her] being and the guardian of [her] virtue"—complete with obscene illustrations, expressions of fanatical morality, and a signature in blood. The juxtaposition of Eleanor's sexual self-hatred and Hugh Crain's teachings has everything to do with what happens between Theodora and Eleanor.

"Your feet are dirty," Theodora says casually, as she paints Eleanor's toenails—and Eleanor panics: "It's *horrible*," she said to Theodora, "it's *wicked*," wanting to cry. Then, helplessly, she began to laugh at the look on Theodora's face . . . I hate having things done to me. . . . I don't like to feel helpless . . . My mother— . . . It's wicked. I mean—on *my* feet. It makes me feel like I look like a fool."

"You've got wickedness and foolishness somehow mixed up," a startled Theodora tells her. In part, of course, she is right. In part, however, she misses the point. Eleanor has been raised in the ideological world of Hugh Crain's precepts; she may surreptitiously buy red clothing, but to glory in her own sexuality, to be a "woman of some color," she would have to be a "different person" indeed. If it is fine for her to do so, what does that say about her entire past? Either such self-indulgence is wicked, or she has been played for a fool.

The message is clear: Eleanor cannot cope with her own sexuality. Henceforth, she will pursue Theodora as an intimate companion, but she will shrink in disgust from her touch. Theodora seems to sense how serious matters are. "You're about as crazy as anyone I ever saw," she says cheerfully at first; and then "gravely," "I have a hunch that you ought to go home." What she cannot know is that Eleanor has no home; and that she, Theodora, has exposed herself as Eleanor's true double, able simultaneously to seduce and annihilate.

—Tricia Lootens, "'Whose Hand Was I Holding?': Familial and Sexual Politics in Shirley Jackson's *The Haunting of Hill House*," in *Haunting the House of Fiction: Feminist Perspectives on Ghost Stories by American Women*, edited by Lynette Carpenter and Wendy K. Kolmar (Knoxville: The University of Tennessee Press, 1991): pp. 184–85.

[Roberta Rubenstein is a professor of Literature at American University. She is the author of *The Novelistic Vision of Doris Lessing: Breaking the Forms of Consciousness,* and *Boundaries of the Self: Gender, Culture, Fiction.* In this excerpt, Rubenstein discusses how Eleanor becomes part of Hill House.]

In Jackson's two final novels, the Gothic pleasure-in-fear that she acknowledged as a driving force in her fiction blends with preoedipal preoccupations to dramatize explicitly not only the ambivalence of the mother-daughter relationship but its figurative expression in consuming houses or other representations of incorporation. In the 1959 novel *The Haunting of Hill House* (a paradigmatic Female Gothic text, according to Kahane), the mother is dead and the daughter is confined within a house that functions figuratively as the externalized maternal body, simultaneously seductive and threatening. The daughter, Eleanor Vance, is drawn to Hill House as a participant in the study of occult phenomena. As Kahane observes,

> from the very beginning the house itself is presented as . . . a maternal antagonist . . . [that singles] out Eleanor as its destined inhabitant. . . . Jackson dislocates [readers] in typical Gothic fashion by locating [us] in Eleanor's point of view, confusing outside and inside, reality and illusion, so that [we] cannot clearly discern the acts of the house—the supernatural—from Eleanor's own disordered acts—the natural. But whether the agency of the house is inside Eleanor's mind or outside it, in either location it clearly functions as a powerful maternal imago.

While Kahane valuably highlights the Female Gothic elements of the narrative, I want to complicate her reading by suggesting that the confusion between inside and outside that structures this novel (and also *We Have Always Lived in the Castle*) is additionally represented through food as literal and symbolic substance. In both narratives, food signals both desire and fear: both the longing for sustenance and the predatory "consume or be consumed" relationship between mother and daughter. Moreover, in these final novels, tensions between opposing elements introduced in the earlier narratives— inside/outside, mother/self, and home/lost—overlap and converge to achieve their fullest representation. For Eleanor Vance of *The Haunting of Hill House*, the mother's death precipitates the daughter's existential homelessness and her literally annihilating experience of being lost: the loss of the self.

Early in the narrative, Eleanor stops at a country restaurant for lunch en route to Hill House for the first time; there she observes a young child who refuses her milk because it is not served in the familiar "cup of stars" from which she is accustomed to drink at home. Eleanor appropriates the image of the child's magical milk cup with its suggestive sense of the mother's absent and idealized nourishment. The very fact that Eleanor never possessed such a cup but makes it hers in imagination, referring to it several times, betrays her distance from and longing for maternal nurturance. However, when Eleanor mentions her recently deceased invalid mother, the association with nourishment is negative. As she explains to Theodora, the other young woman of the group who becomes her confidante, "In my mother's house the kitchen was dark and narrow, and nothing you cooked there ever had any taste or color." The cook who provides food for the guests at Hill House, Mrs. Dudley, prepares delectable dishes, yet is the antithesis of a nurturing figure, utterly mechanical in her insistence on a rigid and undeviating schedule of meals.

Even before the "hauntings" begin, Eleanor is seductively drawn into the house while feeling as if she is being consumed by it, "like a small creature swallowed whole by a monster." When the first manifestation occurs—terrifyingly loud pounding on her door in the night—Eleanor believes it is her dead mother knocking. Later she admits her guilt about the circumstances of her mother's death: "She knocked on the wall and called me . . . and I never woke up." For Theodora, the manifestation of knocking suggested someone trying "to get in and eat us"; in Eleanor's words, "The sense was that it wanted to consume us, take us into itself, make us a part of the house." As Eleanor is progressively incorporated—and infantilized— by the malign powers of Hill House, she feels as if she is quite literally being consumed: "I am disappearing inch by inch into this house, I am going apart a little bit at a time. . . ." The walls of Hill House exude messages intended specifically for Eleanor: "HELP ELEANOR COME HOME." Later the newly arrived Mrs. Montague attempts to communicate with spirits through her "planchette" (Ouija board), which repeatedly produces the words "mother," "child," "lost," and "home."

The meaning of "home" is deeply ironic, and Hill House is indeed both enticing and devouring mother: Eleanor, acknowledging its powerful attraction, *chooses* to "relinquish my possession of this self of mine, abdicate, give over willingly what I never wanted at all; whatever it wants of me it can have." Ultimately, the haunted Eleanor is destroyed by her own ambivalent submission to maternal domination. Of all of Jackson's protagonists, she is most literally consumed by the entrapping/embracing house that overpowers her even as she submits almost joyfully to it. Her assertion, "I am home, I am home . . . ," paired with her conviction that she cannot leave Hill House because "I haven't any [other] home" to return to, vividly exemplifies the convergence of desire and fear in the oppositions inside/outside, mother/self, and home/lost. By the novel's end, Eleanor is dead, having crashed her car into a tree just outside the house in a gesture that may be understood as a suicidal sacrifice to the embracing/consuming mother/house.

—Roberta Rubenstein, "House Mothers and Haunted Daughters: Shirley Jackson and Female Gothic," in *Tulsa Studies in Women's Literature* 15, no. 2 (Fall 1996): pp. 317–19.

Works by
Shirley Jackson

The Road through the Wall. 1948.

The Lottery, or The Adventures of James Harris. 1949.

Hangsaman. 1951.

Life among the Savages. 1953.

The Bird's Nest. 1954.

The Witchcraft of Salem Village. 1956.

Raising Demons. 1957.

The Sundial. 1958.

The Bad Children (play). 1958.

The Haunting of Hill House. 1959.

We Have Always Lived in the Castle. 1962.

Nine Magic Wishes (a children's book). 1963.

The Magic of Shirley Jackson (ed. by Stanley Edgar Hyman). 1966.

Come Along with Me (ed. by Stanley Edgar Hyman). 1968.

Works about
Shirley Jackson

Allen, Barbara. "A Folkloristic Look at Shirley Jackson's 'The Lottery.'" *Tennessee Folklore Society Bulletin* 46 (December 1980): 119–24.

Bagchee, Shyamal. "Design of Darkness in Shirley Jackson's 'The Lottery.'" *Notes on Contemporary Literature* 9, no. 4 (1979): 8–9.

Brooks, Cleanth, and Robert Penn Warren. "'The Lottery': Interpretation." In *Understanding Fiction*, 2nd edition. New York: Appleton-Century-Crofts, 1959.

Carpenter, Lynette. "Domestic Comedy, Black Comedy, and Real Life: Shirley Jackson, a Woman Writer." In *Faith of a (Woman) Writer*, eds. Alice Kessler-Harris and William McBrien. Westport Conn.: Greenwood Press, 1988.

Carpenter, Lynette. "The Establishment and Preservation of Female Power in Shirley Jackson's *We Have Always Lived in the Castle*." *Frontiers* 8, no. 1 (1984): 32–38.

Church, Joseph. "Getting Taken in 'The Lottery.'" *Notes on Contemporary Literature* 18, no. 4 (1988): 10–11.

Cleveland, Carol S. "Shirley Jackson." In *And Then There Were Nine . . . More Women of Mystery*, edited by Jane S. Bakerman. Bowling Green, Ohio: Bowling Green State University Popular Press, 1985.

Coulthard, A. R. "Jackson's 'The Lottery.'" *Explicator* 48, no. 3 (Spring 1990): 226–28.

Downing, Janay. "Much Ado about Nothing: Narrative Strategies in Shirley Jackson and Teresa Bloomingdale." *Whimsy* 1 (1983): 206–08.

Egan, James. "Sanctuary: Shirley Jackson's Domestic and Fantastic Parables." *Studies in Weird Fiction* 6 (1989): 15–24.

Eisinger, Chester E. *Fiction of the Forties.* Chicago: The University of Chicago Press, 1963.

Friedman, Lenemaja. *Shirley Jackson.* Boston: Twayne Publishers, 1975.

Gibson, James M. "An Old Testament Analog for 'The Lottery.'" *Journal of Modern Literature* 11 (March 1984): 193–95.

Hoffman, Steven K. "Individuation and Character Development in the Fiction of Shirley Jackson." *Hartford Studies in Literature* 8, no. 3 (1976): 190–208.

Kittredge, Mary. "The Other Side of Magic: A Few Remarks about Shirley Jackson." In *Discovering Modern Horror Fiction,* edited by Darrell Schweitzer. Mercer Island, Wash.: Starmont House, 1985.

Kosenko, Peter. "A Marxist/Feminist Reading of Shirley Jackson's 'The Lottery.'" *New Orleans Review* 12 (Spring 1985): 27–32.

Lainoff, Seymour. "Jackson's 'The Lottery.'" *Explicator* 12 (March 1954): 34.

Lootens, Tricia. "'Whose Hand Was I Holding?': Familial and Sexual Politics in Shirley Jackson's *The Haunting of Hill House,*" in *Haunting the House of Fiction: Feminist Perspectives on Ghost Stories by American Women,* ed. by Lynette Carpenter and Wendy K. Kolmar. Knoxville, The University of Tennessee Press, 1991.

Nebeker, Helen E. "'The Lottery': Symbolic Tour de Force." *American Literature* 46 (March 1974): 100–107.

Newman, Judie. "Shirley Jackson and the Reproduction of Mothering: *The Haunting of Hill House.*" In *American Horror Fiction: From Brockden Brown to Stephen King,* ed. by Brian Docherty. New York: St. Martin's Press, 1990.

Oehlsclaeger, Fritz. "The Stoning of Mistress Hutchinson: Meaning and Context in 'The Lottery.'" *Essays in Literature* 15 (Fall 1988): 259–65.

Oppenheimer, Judy. *Private Demons: The Life of Shirley Jackson.* New York: Fawcett Columbine, 1988.

Parks, John G. "Chambers of Yearning: Shirley Jackson's Use of the Gothic," in *Twentieth Century Literature* 30, no. 1 (1984): 15–29.

Rubenstein, Roberta. "House Mothers and Haunted Daughters: Shirley Jackson and Female Gothic," *Tulsa Studies in Women's Literature* 15, no. 2 (Fall 1996): 309–332

Schaub, Danielle. "Shirley Jackson's Use of Symbols in 'The Lottery.'" *Journal of the Short Story in English* 14 (Spring 1990): 79–86.

Sullivan, Jack. "Shirley Jackson." In *Supernatural Fiction Writers: Fantasy and Horror,* vol. 2, ed. by E. F. Bleiler. New York: Charles Scribner's Sons, 1985.

Terry, James S., and Peter C. Williams. "Literature and Bioethics: The Tension in Goals and Style." *Literature and Medicine* 7 (1988): 1–21.

Welch, Dennis. "Manipulation in Jackson's 'Seven Types of Ambiguity.'" *Studies in Short Fiction* 18 (Winter 1981): 27–31.

Whittier, Gayle. "'The Lottery' as Misogynist Parable." *Women's Studies* 18, no. 4 (1991): 353-66.

Williams, Richard H. "A Critique of the Sampling Plan Used in Shirley Jackson's 'The Lottery.'" *Journal of Modern Literature* 7 (September 1979): 543–44.

Woodruff, Stuart C. "The Real Horror Elsewhere: Shirley Jackson's Last Novel." *Southwest Review* 52 (Spring 1967): 152–62.

Wylie Hall, Joan. *Shirley Jackson: A Study of the Short Fiction.* New York: Twayne Publishers, 1993.

Index of
Themes and Ideas